Multi-Dimensional Summarization in Cyber-Physical Society

Multi-Dimensional Summarization in Cyber-Physical Society

Hai Zhuge

ELSEVIER

AMSTERDAM • BOSTON • HEIDELBERG • LONDON
NEW YORK • OXFORD • PARIS • SAN DIEGO
SAN FRANCISCO • SINGAPORE • SYDNEY • TOKYO

Elsevier
Radarweg 29, PO Box 211, 1000 AE Amsterdam, Netherlands
The Boulevard, Langford Lane, Kidlington, Oxford OX5 1GB, United Kingdom
50 Hampshire Street, 5th Floor, Cambridge, MA 02139, United States

Notices
Knowledge and best practice in this field are constantly changing. As new research and experience
broaden our understanding, changes in research methods, professional practices, or medical treatment
may become necessary.

Practitioners and researchers must always rely on their own experience and knowledge in evaluating and
using any information, methods, compounds, or experiments described herein. In using such information
or methods they should be mindful of their own safety and the safety of others, including parties for
whom they have a professional responsibility.

To the fullest extent of the law, neither the Publisher nor the authors, contributors, or editors, assume any
liability for any injury and/or damage to persons or property as a matter of products liability, negligence
or otherwise, or from any use or operation of any methods, products, instructions, or ideas contained in
the material herein.

Library of Congress Cataloging-in-Publication Data
A catalog record for this book is available from the Library of Congress

British Library Cataloguing-in-Publication Data
A catalogue record for this book is available from the British Library

ISBN: 978-0-12-803455-2

For Information on all Elsevier publications
visit our website at https://www.elsevier.com

Working together
to grow libraries in
developing countries

www.elsevier.com • www.bookaid.org

Publisher: Todd Green
Acquisition Editor: Todd Green
Editorial Project Manager: Lindsay Lawrence
Production Project Manager: Priya Kumaraguruparan
Designer: Matthew Limbert

Typeset by MPS Limited, Chennai, India

Dedicated to my father Zhang Zhuge who passed away when I was writing this book.

I would like to use the following picture to represent a memorial to him

Field of Poppies, 1890 by Vincent van Gogh.

Contents

About the Author

Hai Zhuge has been named a Distinguished Scientist by the Association of Computing Machinery (ACM), in recognition of "significant accomplishments in, and impact on, the computing field." He has made systematic contributions to semantics modeling and advanced cyber-infrastructure, for efficiently sharing knowledge through lasting fundamental innovation on knowledge, semantics, dimension and self-organization. He pioneers research toward Cyber-Physical Society with methodological, theoretical and technical innovations as well as typical applications.

Foreword

It is a pleasure to write a foreword to Hai Zhuge's new book and to welcome him to the UK as a colleague, as he takes up his chair at Aston University. Within the wider Semantic Web research project, I think Hai Zhuge is trying to do something bold and important: first, by asking how can big data, and all that the movement now entails, be made to yield up representations that give us some understanding of the content implicit in the data, that is not essentially textual. This is his Resource Space Model, a multi-dimensional category space that uniformly represents human understanding and the patterns in real and abstract objects. Secondly, he is asking how can we have a common representation for the content of different modalities: not just speech and text but images and 3D objects, the long-awaited Internet of Things. He then takes summarization as a reasonably well-understood task environment where the notion of summarization beyond the textual, the standard case so far, can be explored and ultimately tested. I think he is asking serious and fundamental questions in this work and proposing bold research solutions. This is an important issue in the history of idea development of the semantic web where many have transitioned seamlessly from the term "semantic web" to the "data web," without always thinking of what that entails. For example, the whole motivation of the semantic web was to have a web of understandable meanings or interpretations that the WWW of texts did not have; it was humans reading the texts who supplied the interpretations. The shift to a "data web" downplays that notion of comprehensible or cognitive content and it is that, that Hai Zhuge wants to put back. I salute the ambitious nature of his research goals that this book sets out.

Yorick Wilks
IHMC, Pensacola and Ocala, FL, United States
University of Sheffield, Sheffield, United Kingdom
23 May 2016

Preface

Realizing expert-level automatic summarization has been a dream of computing. This work was initiated from the following self-observations when I was traveling in America in October 2012.

The first observation is that our minds often merge image-like representations when reading texts relevant to experience, such as news and novels. We also talk and write according to the images in the mind. The recall of the images in the mind accompanies the reorganization of mental space. This indicates that the human mind is likely to have the mechanism that can uniformly process various forms of representation and use one form of representation to interpret the other form of representation. The following question emerges when linking this observation to the problem of summarization: Can we realize a general summarization method through modeling a human information processing mechanism?

The second observation is that we can use our own words when making a summarization. This indicates that humans make summarizations with the knowledge for understanding and the knowledge of using language. The following question arises when linking this observation to the problem of summarization: Can we explore the summarization problem from some basic structures and behaviors involved in language use and understanding?

The third observation is that humans can make creative summarizations with knowledge and reasoning. Long-term experience in physical space enables humans to gain the ability to observe and think through different dimensions. People become more insightful when they can observe and think through more dimensions with deeper structure. The following question emerges when linking this observation to the problem of summarization: Can we explore summarization in a multi-dimensional space to enable summarization systems to summarize from different dimensions?

The fourth observation is that humans are living in a complex space consisting of cyberspace, physical space and social space, which evolves with human endeavors to develop science and technology. The development of 3D/4D printers and 3D/4D display devices provides a new condition for displaying summary. The following question emerges when linking this observation to the problem of summarization: Can we explore the summarization problem in a Cyber-Physical-Social space rather than in the text space to realize the Summarization of Things?

The major problems of traditional text summarization approaches are too specific to apply to various forms of text, and the rationality of summarization processes is neglected. I was thinking of developing a rational approach, such that summary can be derived from a given text through a reasoning process, based on user requirement and a set of rules. The advantage is that the summarization can suit any requirement and the summarization process is interpretable. However, it is hard without a formal definition of summarization, and this has been neglected in this research area.

It is critical for summarization research to identify boundaries.

The first research boundary is to develop a computing process that can generate a piece of text from the original text according to a set of predefined rules and constraints. This type of research just needs to be concerned with the rationality of the rules and the efficiency of the computing process. The computing result can be for humans to read or for application systems to use. It is not necessary to evaluate the automatic summarization by comparing the result with the result of human summarization because the computing process is different from the human thinking process in nature. The result of summarization can be the input of various application systems or for human users to quickly know the interested contents.

The second research boundary is to develop an intelligent summarization system that aims at human-level summarization. Solving this problem requires the intelligent summarization system to have the same level of knowledge and cognitive ability as human experts. It is hard to reach this goal by just improving the computing process.

Realizing an intelligent summarization concerns the following fundamental scientific problems:

(1) Modeling human-level knowledge, understanding and representation.
(2) Multi-dimensional semantic computing, which can zoom-in and zoom-out through multiple dimensions on the representations of different levels according to the rules of different dimensions.
(3) The intrinsic relations between representation, semantics, computing and knowledge.

Solving these problems needs to coordinate the knowledge of multiple fields including, language, cognition, and psychology, through the insight of the trend of computing. Research within this boundary needs to consider the human dimension and other dimensions. Research concerns philosophical thoughts and methodologies but does not discuss whether the system has the same level of intelligence as a human or not, because this involves another boundary of research on the nature of human and machine.

The third research boundary is the philosophy about knowledge, intelligence, dimension, and Cyber-Physical Society on summarization. This book does not focus on research within this boundary.

I hope this book can inspire innovation within this area and beyond, and make a significant contribution to the transformation of the research paradigm in the age of the scientific, societal, and industrial revolution.

Hai Zhuge
29 May 2016

Acknowledgment

I would like to take this opportunity to thank Aston University and the Chinese Academy of Sciences for providing a collaborative research environment for me to carry out this fundamental research. I sincerely thank the great painters of the artworks that I used in this book. I sincerely thank my family's continuous support through my career. Thanks go to the ACM Distinguished Speaker Program, which supported me in getting invited to deliver lectures on this topic at a number of international conferences, research institutes and universities in Africa, Asia, America and Europe. Thanks also go to my colleagues and students for their support and cooperation. The earlier research work was supported by the National Science Foundation of China.

Introduction

1

To realize an expert-level automatic summarization is a challenge to computing research [49]. *Automatic summarization has been studied for over a half century, following the traditional paradigm of computing. It is now critical to shift research paradigm with the emerging Cyber-Physical Society and the revolution of sciences, technologies, and industries. Observing various human summaries and rethinking how human make summaries is a way to inspire fundamental research.*

Versatile summaries accompany our daily life. People have created many forms of summary such as the abstracts of scientific papers, the prefaces of books, the tables of contents, personal curriculum vitae, the headlines of news, webpages with hyperlinks, book reviews, Wikipedia, and the results of Web search. Some summaries incorporate pictures, videos, graphs, or tables into texts. Applications include Web portals such as Yahoo, YouTube, posters, slides, medical certificates, TV guides, advertisements, and conference programs. A good summary should represent the core meaning of the original text, quickly attract attention, and effectively convey meaning with regard to interests. The current summaries that people often read are designed by professional people.

1.1 Open collaborative human summarization

Wikipedia can be regarded as an open collaborative human summarization environment. One Wikipedia page is a summary of one thing. Figure 1.1 shows a Wikipedia page that summarizes John McCarthy, the pioneer of artificial intelligence. It looks like a Web-style curriculum vitae. From the other pages on events and concepts, we can see that Wikipedia uses a set of structures similar to book (e.g., table of contents) and paper (e.g., begin with a definition, followed by historical review, and ended with references, further readings and external links) to unify various content contributions and help readers to understand the entries with reading experience.

The advantages of Wikipedia can be summarized as follows:

1. *The representation adopts the language structure that appears in books, papers, and webpages.* It is in line with human reading experience. The table of contents with hyperlinks guides readers to read the interested parts quickly. The reference links provide supportive or extended reading materials for readers. Different from the structures of the hardcopy newspapers, books and papers, its structure is suitable for Web browsing.

2. *The content of its page is divided by sections* (with title), which helps readers' understanding through the structure and divides the interests of contributors. Sections are relatively independent from each other, which enables different contributors to focus on different sections at one time of contribution and to represent various viewpoints from different aspects of understandings.

Multi-Dimensional Summarization in Cyber-Physical Society. DOI: http://dx.doi.org/10.1016/B978-0-12-803455-2.00001-9

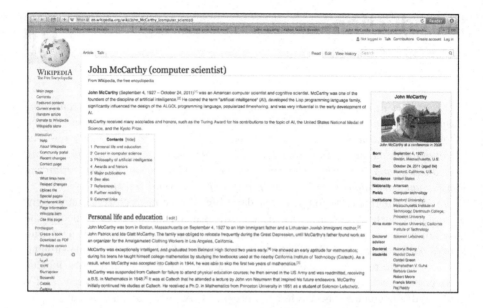

Figure 1.1 Wikipedia: a Web-based platform for collaborative human summarization.

3. *It opens to all users to read and edit.* This openness enables the contents to evolve to reflect various viewpoints and understandings from different contributors at different times.
4. *It has a category network on pages.* A category with attributes id, page-id, name, in-links, out-links, and pages provides the links for browsing the pages within a category or through categories. Figure 1.2 is an example of the category network. Different from the traditional category hierarchy that makes accurate classification and represents a single abstraction, the category network has loops so that the links between categories do not just represent single abstraction. This reflects diverse understandings of contributors and can help establish more possible links between terms in other texts if terms can be mapped into categories.
5. *It provides an evolving common content base and indicates the ways to make abstraction for interpreting terms.* The contents are for human to read while the category network guides people to browse relevant contents. The category network provides indicators for various application systems to predict and suggest abstraction approach.

Wikipedia has the following shortcomings, especially from the computing point of view:

1. The size and display of the content cannot adapt to the interests of different readers.
2. It usually takes a long time to evolve into a complete content of a page. This leads to incomplete content and redundant links and categories.

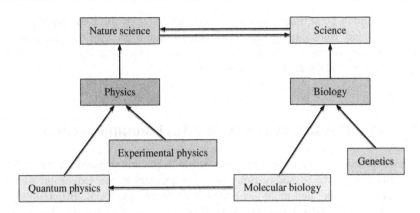

Figure 1.2 A category network in Wikipedia, where the arrows point to super-categories.

3. It relies on human contribution and labor-intensive editing work.
4. The category structure is not strong enough in structure and semantics (e.g., the current attributes of category do not reflect the nature of the category in question) to explain representation and reflect abstraction. A well-structured and semantics-rich category hierarchy can better explain representations from different abstraction levels, e.g., explaining two representations with the following keyword sets "I, like, apple" and "He, like, orange" by a representation at the higher abstraction level "People, like, fruit."
5. It can help readers to understand some terms explained in natural language, but it is limited in ability to interpret diverse representations, and it is also hard to interpret a summarization result and the process of summarization since the purpose of designing the category structure is to provide navigational links to all of its pages in a hierarchy of categories which enables readers who know "essential—defining—characteristics" of a topic to browse and quickly find the sets of pages on topics with the characteristics.
6. It lacks objective evaluation on the contents and categories, which can provide significant guidance for contributors and readers.

The Wikipedia is a platform that enables people to make and share a collaborative summarization on the World Wide Web. It records users' understandings and opinions and evolves with operations. The following chapters will discuss the applications of Wikipedia.

A way to obtain the interpretation of representation (e.g., a term in text) is to map the representation into the categories in Wikipedia by using one language representation to interpret another language representation. One advantage of the mapping is that it can save people's time for searching the interpretations of a representation. The limitation is that it is not formalized for machines to carry out reasoning to prove a solution or verify an assumption strictly. Therefore, the interpretation is empirical and incomplete. On the other hand, Wikipedia mainly contains general and mature categories, so it is not able to interpret specific categories, especially the new concepts appeared in research like the concept of Cyber-Physical Society. From the evolution point of view, Wikipedia will include more and more categories. New concepts will be included in Wikipedia later when they become common-interest concepts. However the expression ability of

Wikipedia cannot be stronger than the natural language as the basic representation components and rules are a subset of natural language. Besides the category network, Wikipedia can be analogy to short survey papers, which summarize the concepts, history, methods, and opinions.

1.2   The necessity of automatic text summarization

The development of cyberspace (with prosperous applications based on the Internet, communication networks and various devices) accelerates the expansion of texts since people can more and more easily and freely publish writings. Efficiently finding necessary contents in the ocean of texts is very important because life is short while new texts are continually generated.

With the development of sciences, more and more papers and books are published. Innovation requests researchers to read more and more publications to know the status of research, but researchers are limited in time and energy to read the constantly generated publications. Researchers have to select a small part of papers to read with some strategies, e.g., selecting the latest papers that usually review more recent works or selecting the highly cited papers that influence an area. This leads to more and more reinventions because some old papers are important, some across-area work are excluded from search scope, and the closely related papers may not be highly cited for some reasons. Original innovation, especially systematic and fundamental innovation, becomes more and more difficult with the rapid expansion of papers.

One solution to solve the above problem is to build an e-science environment, which can use all computing techniques and recommend the necessary publications or relevant reference contents to appropriate researchers who are working on relevant areas, or recommend inspiring or complementary contents to appropriate researchers while they are thinking. This means it is required for the e-science environment to know the interests of researchers, which may be reflected by their publications, homepages, browsing behaviors, and search behaviors.

In the future, an advanced e-science environment will be able to estimate interests according to the current interests, the pattern of research development, and the emerging topics.

Automatic summarization is another effort, which can provide a concise content for researchers. Researchers have made great efforts to realize this dream. However, existing approaches are empirical and focus on special types of text. It is necessary to review previous efforts and explore the foundation of summarization.

There are different definitions of text summarization. The common point is regarding text summarization as an automatic process of distilling the most important language representation components like sentences from a text to produce an abridged version for a particular task and user [74,75].

The generic summarizers usually generate important contents in text(s) without considering readers. The query-focused summarizers generate responses to user queries. The extractive summarizers select appropriate phrases or sentences from the text and then compose them, using different (probably more general) words to represent the main meaning of text. The query-focused summarization usually works with the extractive summarization and generic summarization. So far, most text summarizers are extractive. It is more technically feasible to extract sentences according to statistical analysis and experience on the text to be summarized. Making abstraction needs knowledge on and even beyond the text. It is an effect of social selection of research.

Automatic text summarization systems generally concern the following three issues:

1. *Selection.* Scan and select the important language components (e.g., sentences) from source text according to some measures.
2. *Ordering.* Determine the order of the selected components.
3. *Composition.* Compose the selected components to get a new text, where components should be organized for understanding easily.

1.3   Practice in search engines

The current search engines are incorporating text summarization into displaying search results. Google makes a short text summarization of the most important item and places the summary at the head of the list of search results in response to the queries, for example "dentist salary UK" as shown in Figure 1.3. Although no technical details have been reported so far, it is likely to make the summary by extracting sentences containing the keyword "salary" from the Web page about a UK dentist's salary and organizing summary according to the identification of the purpose of the query. The example regards the purpose of the query as searching the salary of dentist in the UK. As keywords will likely indicate diverse meanings, the summary may not satisfy some users. For example, the query purpose may be to know the dentists' salary outside the UK or the dentists getting salary in the UK.

Google is developing the technique to make summarization by extracting objects. Figures 1.3–1.6 show the summaries for object queries. Figure 1.4 shows the result of a summarization embedded in the search result in response to query on "v. bush." The search engine is likely to make the summary as follows: (1) determine the type of the object (in this example, "v.bush" is identified as a person, V. Bush); (2) select the template of the object (e.g., person) from a template base; (3) extract sentences from the source about the features of the object (including time, name, and relevant persons) from the text; and, (4) organize the summary as a list consisting of the representation of the object that includes a brief introduction of the features, which are likely the common concern of the users of the search engine. In this example, the source is from Wikipedia and features include the date of birth, the date of death, the persons who are influenced, parents, children, links to the relevant books, and the people also search for.

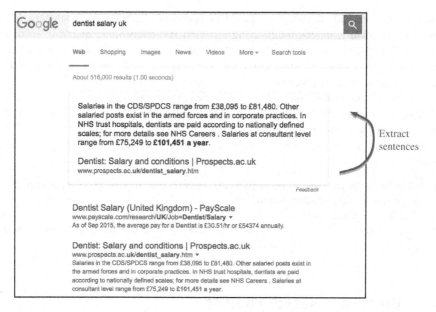

Figure 1.3 Query-based summarization by extracting sentences.

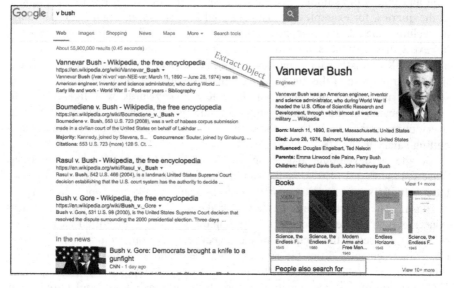

Figure 1.4 Query-based summarization by extracting the features of the queried object according to the type of object and the relevant template.

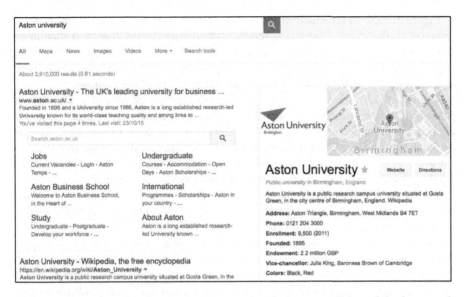

Figure 1.5 Query-based summarization by extracting the important links and the features of the queried object.

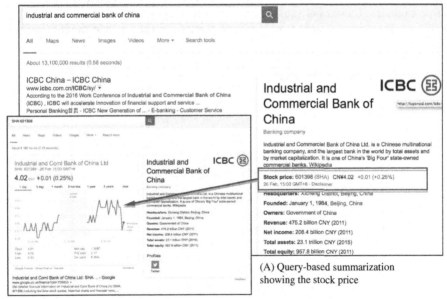

(A) Query-based summarization showing the stock price

(B) The summary extended from the link about the stock quotes extracted from Reuters

Figure 1.6 Query-based summarization showing dynamic data.

Figure 1.5 shows the result of a summarization embedded in the search result in response to the query "Aston University." In addition to the object extraction as shown in Figure 1.4, it extracts the important links from the homepage of the object with simple summary and displays its location on the map. This provides more aspects about the searched object for the searchers to know at a glimpse.

Figure 1.6 (A) shows the result of a summarization embedded in the search result in response to the query "industrial and commercial bank of China." The difference is that the features of the object include a presentation of the stock price of the bank with a link. Clicking the link shows the chart of the quotes of the stock extracted as shown in Figure 1.6 (B). The source of the summary of the object (bank) is from Wikipedia and the source of the quotes is from Reuters.

This observation indicates that summarization has moved beyond text and used human summarization results like Wikipedia pages. Google only makes summaries for some objects because it is difficult for the empirical method to cover all possible queries. However, it is significant for users to read the summaries for those important objects (e.g., those with advertisements or high click rate) at first glimpse.

Figure 1.7 shows the result of a summarization embedded in the search result of Google in response to the query "from Birmingham to Giza." The result shows that it regards the purpose of the query as knowing the flights between two cities. The time of duration, the carrier and the number of stops are likely the main concern of querying flight. The result relies on the experience of designers and available data of past queries. It does not satisfy users when their query purposes are about wind, will, and distance. Different from previous displays, it uses a table to represent the

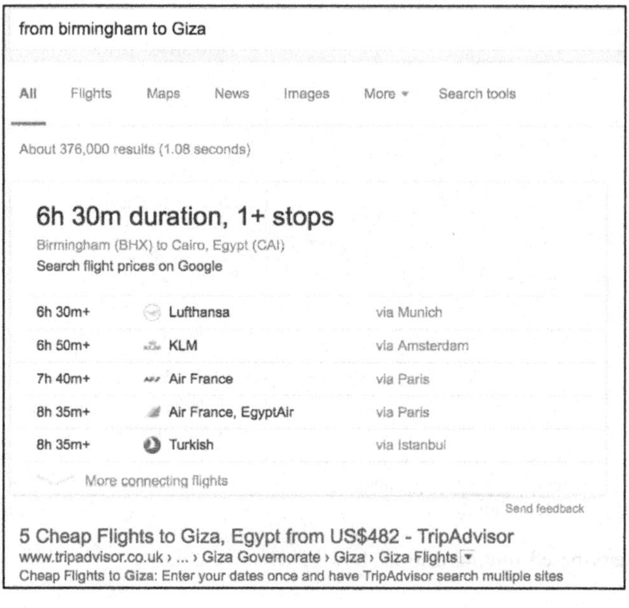

Figure 1.7 Use table to represent summary.

summary. It is an empirical way to facilitate readers' understanding to use a widely understandable form to display summary especially in particular areas because there is no universal form to suit all cases.

1.4   Practice in e-science: summarizing multiple scientific papers through citation

The rapid development of information technology—especially the Internet—enables people to conveniently communicate, study, research, and work. One of the consequences is that more and more texts are generated. On the other hand, human life and reading time have not been significantly extended. The ocean of texts is increasing the difficulty for effectively sharing information. Researchers are usually only able to read a part of the papers that are necessary for research. That is, *research is conducted in an incomplete and evolving environment*, which leads to essentially repeat research. E-science is a way to overcome this difficulty.

One of the applications of text summarization is to summarize scientific papers. It is significant for researchers to save the time for searching papers relevant to their research and the time for reading the full papers. It is feasible because scientific papers have two characteristics: well-structured and explicit citation, which represents the opinions from the author(s).

Citations in the same representation component (like sentence or paragraph) are usually about the same thing, called "common fact" in [18], for example, the citation representation "*Information retrieval.* Features such as the frequency of word and phrase, location, and rank of sentence were used to extract important sentences [11,29]" is about the common thing indicated by the terms "information retrieval," "frequency of word and phrase," "location," "rank sentence," and "extract important sentences."

One significant application of summarization is to summarize the references of an interested paper so that a reader can quickly know the related work without searching and reading the references while reading the paper. As a paper may only cite a part of a reference, making use of the citation representations within the paper is a way to make an appropriate summarization according to the intentions of the author(s) when writing the paper.

Summarization can carry out by detecting the common things and making use of the common things to select the candidate sentences from the reference papers for composing the summary. A set of common things may be distributed in different locations within a paper. One problem needs to be solved first is that citations may not use the same terms to render the common thing. An empirical solution is to develop a term-association discovering mechanism to expand terms based on a large set of abstracts of papers, which ensures the wide coverage of the terms. Figure 1.8 depicts the basic idea of the system, which extracts common things by selecting the citation sentences and clustering these sentences.

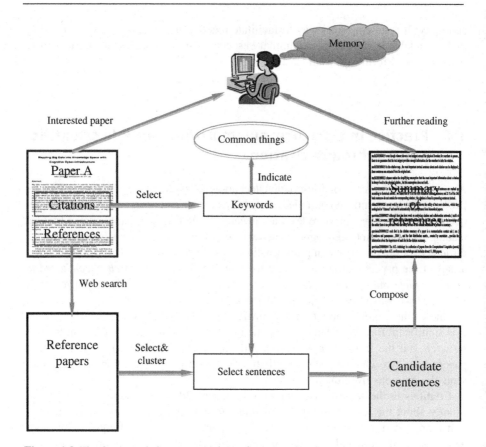

Figure 1.8 The framework for summarizing references of an interested paper.

When observing the process of human text understanding, memory plays an important role. The following is the basic process of understanding text:

1. Locate the first interested representation within a paper.
2. Recall the interpretation of the representation in memory. The interpretation can be the definition of the representation, that is, the related representations through semantic links (e.g., the cause-effect link).
3. If the interpretation can be found in memory or can be interpreted by the existing representations in memory, the reader understands the current representation and continues to locate the next representation.
4. Otherwise the reader has to search and read the references and then to locate the relevant representations to interpret the current representation.

An automatic summarization system can significantly help with step (4). The left hand side of the up part of Figure 1.9 (A) shows an output of the summarization on a common thing, which further explains the citation representation of the reading paper although it is not as fluent as human summarization. This could greatly save the time for readers when reading a paper, especially reading an across-area paper where many new concepts need to be interpreted.

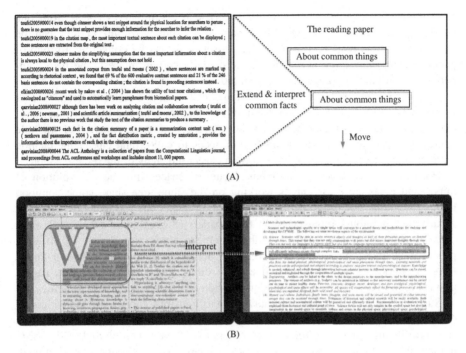

(A)

(B)

Figure 1.9 (A) A summary of the references on the citation representations. It extends and interprets the common things while reading. (B) An illustrative interface for implementing the system.

The above observation inspires a summarization system that can automatically generate the real-time interpretation while reading a paper:

1. Build a memory space to represent user's research interest by collecting the user's own papers and all the references, the papers that cited the user's papers, the papers that have been browsed and downloaded, and the keywords that were used to search papers.
2. Locate an appropriate window for the representation of the common things that need to be interpreted according to the memory space because not all common things need to be interpreted. To do this, the representations need to be ranked according to the memory space.
3. Search the reference papers according to the citation representations, and search the papers that cited the reading paper.
4. Select the relevant representations within the search results.
5. Summarize the relevant representations as the interpretation of the representation to be interpreted.
6. Do (2) until the end of the paper.

Figure 1.9 (B) is an illustrative interface for implementing the system. It shows the usefulness in helping reader to quickly locate and understand some special representations when reading a paper.

This work can be extended from explicit citation to implicit citation, which is often used in other forms of texts like literature and news. The key step is to find the relevant texts and locate the representation that needs to be interpreted by comparing the reading text with the memory space.

From application point of view, this work can be further extended from one reading paper to a set of interested papers. A summarization system can be extended to guide readers to quickly read a set of papers by collecting a group of papers on the same topic according to the reader's current interest, and then compare different views on the same representations.

The system can be also extended to automatically search a set of interested papers from the Web according to user's memory and then recommend not only the interested papers but also the summary of the references of those papers. For multiple interested papers, the summarization system needs to collect and cluster the citation representations among those papers to form a cluster hierarchy of the representations.

Humans have created an enormous document space with the co-evolution of minds and cyberspace. Scientists working on the same area share some common things (including common assumptions, common data, common methods, common or different opinions) represented in their papers. Surveying relevant work is to actually categorize and summarize the common things represented in different papers. It is more significant to summarize documents based on common things through citation. The formatted and explicit citation features of scientific papers provide a good condition for the implementation of the summarization system.

Such an interest directed summarization is feasible and can help readers to quickly know more relevant work. If a friendly interface can be developed, this can significantly save the time of researchers who have to search and read a large number of cited papers, especially for new researchers. If appropriately designed, the summarization system may help a reader to have a quick impression on all references of an interested theme. Further, the summarization of references leads to the literature reviews of research. For many papers, a classification of common things helps make the summarization of common and different ideas in literature.

An advanced summarization system should be able to provide some inspiration for readers. This requests the summarization system to establish the mappings between citations and the mappings between the things indicated by common citations and to establish an analogical reasoning mechanism based on these mappings to provide imaginative suggestions. Analogical reasoning on semantic link network is a way to generate conjectures on potential semantic links [141].

A smart summarization system should be able to summarize the development of an area along the expansion of the citation network and the common and different interests of scientists and practitioners to predict the emerging research themes. A research theme emerges not only with the development of science and technology but also with the development of society, including culture, economy, policy, and environment. Therefore, a summarization system should be integrated into a Cyber-Physical-Social e-science environment to effectively support scientific research, planning, decision and assessment.

The current open big data movement makes it possible to detect the coherence between the development of science and the development of society.

Chapter 8 General citation, will further discuss the relationship between citation and summarization. Chapter 16 Creative summarization, will further discuss an interest-led reading model.

1.5 A multi-dimensional perspective of summarization literature

A dimension represents a view of observation. The recognition of dimension is the basis of establishing spaces. From an algebraic point of view, a dimension represents a method of partitioning a set. Different dimensions represent different partitioning methods.

Research on automatic text summarization started half century ago [11,69]. Research methods can be summarized in a multi-dimensional category space [134,141], as shown in Figure 1.10, where every point in the space coordinates all methods specified at every dimension. A dimension can be a hierarchy of categories, where every point corresponds to a coordinate as in a distance space.

Methods can be classified by input and output. There are three types of inputs: (1) *single text* [69], (2) *multiple texts* [77] [2,84,98], and (3) hybrid, which inputs one text and retrieves multiple relevant texts and then summarizes them so that readers can know more relevant contents. It is useful in summarizing a scientific theme [95] [18].

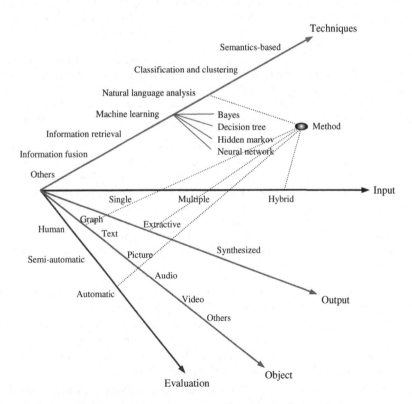

Figure 1.10 A multi-dimensional category space of summarization methods.

There are two types of outputs: (1) *extractive summarization* (extracting and composing important sentences from the given text) [29,80,108], and (2) *synthesized summarization* (summarization is a reformulated, compressed, abstracted, or synthesized text) [57,78]. Sentences in output should be coherent to facilitate reading [10,13]. Methods can also be categorized by techniques as follows:

1. *Information fusion.* Summary is generated by identifying the themes in text and selecting appropriate sentences for composition [8,9].
2. *Information retrieval.* Features such as the frequency of word and phrase, location, and rank of sentence were used to extract the important sentences [11,29].
3. *Machine learning.* Machine learning methods are applied statistical techniques to extractive summarization, including Bayes Methods [26,58,67], rich features and decision trees [64], Markov Models [23], Neural Networks [85], classification [92,115], and hybrid machine learning method [34].
4. *Natural language analysis.* Methods for extracting the features of text based on natural language analysis were used in summarization, including word distribution [69], cue phrase like "in conclusion" and the location information (e.g., sentences in headings, beginning and end, and in bold) [29], extracting significant sentences by identifying the lexical chain in text [7,109]), and computing the important sentence in a graph representation of sentences [33a,145].
5. *Classification and clustering.* Classification and clustering are the basic components of the multi-document summarization methods. It is usually used with graph analysis and information retrieval [33a,52]. Applications include summarizing positive and negative classifications within texts [55,92].
6. *Semantics-based.* Cognition scientists simulated human reading and understanding process as a series of propositions input and reduction cycles [14,56]. Text understanding is modeled by proposition network. The latent semantic analysis technique was used to identify semantically important sentences. Summarization patterns were discussed [43]. Discovering semantic communities or some semantic structures is a way to summarize a network of language components [138].
7. *Other methods*, including *information extraction* (extracting entities, relations, and structures), *document compression, ranking method* [15,25,100], *probabilistic approaches* [57,96], and *citation-based approaches* [4,30]. The faceted navigation approach does not belong to traditional text summarization, but it can be regarded as a special summarization because it can extract multiple facets in large text(s) to enable users to read only the interested facet [129]. Furthermore, the facets can be developed into dimensions with multiple abstraction levels. Similarly, the association relation between words was used for multi-document summarization [47]. The approach to summarizing the differences between document groups was studied [123].

Existing methods provide experience and components for creating new methods. The multi-dimensional category space helps specify, organize, understand, manage and use the existing methods and invent new methods. The category hierarchy of the method space evolves with operations. Different methods (e.g., information retrieval and natural language analysis) can be integrated to construct a complex method or updated as a new category in the category hierarchy.

Evaluation concerns human, semi-automatic and automatic methods based on the pre-defined standards [74]. The methods for creating summaries and the methods for evaluating summaries are closely related [51].

Summarization research has been done on multi-medias and social events with multi-media features. Summarizing videos is a research theme in multimedia area [28] [32]. Some social events can be detected and summarized with the wide use of online social networks [144]. To investigate the relationships between different summarization methods is a way to make generalization.

Human text summarization is based on language understanding, which is a research area of psychology. Information processing in reading was early modeled by visual information transformation through a series of processing stages involving visual, phonological, and episodic memory systems until it is finally comprehended in the semantic system [59]. The mechanisms of mental operations that underlie the processes occurring in text comprehension and in the production of recall and summarization protocols were investigated [56]. Psychological research provides another dimension for exploring text summarization through simulating human text understanding.

Cognitive science provides another dimension to understand text summarization. An intelligent text summarization system can benefit from cognitive research. For example, recognition about the roles of cause and reason: Readers tend to prefer rational interpretations of actions when human or human-like agents are involved in analysis but tend to prefer causal interpretations when nonhuman are concerned. Readers know the current state of the system and the changes involved in the causes and reasons, and tend to find instances to test them. Some researchers argued that more complex taxonomy beyond causes and reasons are not necessary [126].

A concept that has been neglected in text summarization area is the preference semantics system, which is for extracting the meaning and structure of natural language texts, based on some notions such as maximal semantic density and coherence, and considering the trade-off between representational expressiveness for tractability [124,125].

1.6 Characteristics of text summarization

Existing research methods have the following characteristics:

1. *From text to text.* The main focus of existing research is on text itself. It is a natural idea to select and organize important sentences from the original text to make a summary. Researchers pursue the natural representation of language. Unfortunately, researchers do not achieve a satisfied result. A different opinion is that language representations (e.g., words and sentences) are the indicators of semantics rather than semantics, and interaction plays an important role in the process of representation and understanding [139]. And, the knowledge for summarization is often beyond text. For example, "A love story" is the high-level summarization of a novel, but the word "story" may not be an important word in the novel or it even does not appear in the novel. Why can human use the words beyond text? An explanation is that human have semantic link networks of concepts in minds [140]. Concepts are linked to experiences and language representations. A concept can link to one word or multiple words. A word like "novel" is linked to another word like "story" through one concept or two linked concepts. Therefore, people can emerge "story" when they read a word "novel." When many people have built some common semantic link networks of concepts in minds, commonsense is generated. Humans use common sense to make summarizations that are beyond the ability of previous summarization systems.

2. *Empirical.* It is natural to make use of human experience like the location of particular words to implement automatic summarization. Adding a ground with more indicators to a summary is a way to help representation and understanding, e.g., "A love story in Qing Dynasty of China" includes a time indicator "Qing Dynasty" and a location indicator "China." Empirical approaches are useful in some particular areas like summarizing scientific papers, but the application scope of such methods is narrow. Statistic methods reflect the features (e.g., distribution of words) of text rather than semantics.

3. *Automation.* A summarization system was regarded as an automatic computing process that inputs text and outputs summary according to a predesigned program. In contrast, human summarization involves in operations on knowledge space in mind while reading and writing in natural languages. Human experience with representations, understanding and summarization at multiple levels in lifetime. Human summarization is not a traditional computing problem.

4. *Closed system.* The process of automatic summarization does not interact with other processes in cyberspace and social space where readers and writers live and work to develop the culture that evolves languages and influences the way of understanding. In fact, reviews and comments (e.g., on a hotel's services) in cyberspace are open, easily available, and valuable for composing and improving summaries. For example, different researchers' comments on a paper reflect the understanding of the paper from different perspectives so can be used to generate a summary with multiple perspectives. Customers' comments on a hotel can be categorized to help generate the summary of a hotel from multiple perspectives.

1.7 Requirement from enterprise content computing and big data

1.7.1 Enterprise content computing

Enterprise content computing concerns the strategies, methods, and tools for the management of the lifecycle of the contents generated from various activities of enterprises, which record and help manage the execution of the whole enterprise processes. Using the state-of-the-art information techniques, enterprise content computing transforms business models toward content-centered business models. Enterprise content computing aims at adding values to business with content computing platforms that support data analytics, process management and optimization, decision with insight, and customer engagement. This action is in line with the challenge of big data and the fourth industrial revolution.

Enterprise content computing solutions like IBM serve to capture, transform, deliver, and govern the contents generated in enterprises with the following practices:

1. *Content management,* which is to capture and manage contents to provide access to any device for efficient execution of enterprises.

2. *Advanced case management,* which is to activate contents and incorporate them into the business processes to enhance efficiency, to reduce errors, and to improve responsive quality to customers.

3. *Information lifecycle governance,* which is to analyze information and apply policy consistently across organization to lower cost and risk while increasing the value of contents.

Summarization is one of the techniques that can help realize efficient enterprise content management. It can play the following roles:

1. Summarizing the increasing volume of the internal contents that record material flow, information flow, and money flow through enterprises.
2. Summarizing huge external contents (about suppliers, customers and market) according to the requirements of different roles such as CEO, line managers, and customers.
3. Summarization is desirable to save the time of users who play different roles in enterprises. For example, it enables customers to know more about the enterprises and products.

The content of enterprise concerns versatile documents (e.g., the orders of purchasing raw materials or sales), tables (e.g., the records of warehouse and customers), images (e.g., photos of products), videos (e.g., advertisements and monitoring records for production and security), etc. These applications request summarization methods to apply not only to texts but also to tables, images, and videos.

A multi-dimensional category space coordinates human's multi-dimensional understanding and the multi-dimensional patterns in various resources [141]. Putting summarization into the multi-dimensional category space is a way to obtain insight on various resources.

1.7.2 Big data

Big data research has attracted great attention in science, technology, industry, and society. It is developing with the evolving science paradigm, the transformational innovation of technologies, the fourth industrial revolution, and the transformation of society.

IBM's big data initiative is to integrate current techniques such as content computing, database, and stream processing and to upgrade enterprise information systems toward higher performance and better services for enterprise management and decision. The content management research enables comprehensive content lifecycle and document management with cost-effective control of existing and new types of content with scale, security and stability. This enterprise computing strategy significantly upgrades enterprise information systems (http://www.ibm.com/big-data). This is the significant extension of traditional techniques for integrating, organizing and managing data from multiple sources for supporting estimation and decision.

Data science aims at deriving valuable insights or knowledge from big data. Insights from big data enable enterprises to make better decisions in deepening customer engagement, optimizing operations, etc. Researchers from various disciplines such as statistics, business, social science, communication, and computer science are investigating big data from various aspects such as modeling, analysis, mining, management and utilization. Predictive knowledge helps make insightful decision in business applications.

The converging effort from multiple disciplines and diverse communities is becoming an important driving force for pushing forward big data research. The idea of mapping big data into knowledge space through representations of different levels was introduced in [143]. Summarization of big data is a key solution to obtaining interested representations from big data, especially the rapidly expanding online texts, image, and videos.

1.8 Shifting paradigm

Many areas such as information retrieval, recommendation, query answering, text classification, and text clustering have significantly influenced summarization research. The research paradigm of summarization adopts the research paradigm of those relevant areas, which generally follow the empirical research stream in the computing field. Texts are regarded as the data input for computing, which outputs text as static data through a pre-designed program. Evaluation relies on a set of selected data.

The current text summarization approaches are too specific to apply to various forms of text, and the interpretability of the summarization processes is very low. One way is to develop a rational method such that a summary can be derived from a given text through a reasoning process, based on some assumptions, user requirement, and a set of rules. Formally, $text = f$ (*Text, Rules, Reasoning, Assumption, Requirement*), where f maps the input *Text* into the output *text through reasoning according to the rules*. The advantage is that the summarization suits any requirement and the summarization process is interpretable. However, it is still hard if we do not clear what is summarization.

It is significant for summarization research to identify the following two research boundaries:

1. Develop a computing process that can generate a piece of text from the original text according to a set of predefined rules and constraints for terminating the process. This type of research just needs to concern the rationality of the rules and the efficiency of computing process. It is not necessary to compare the summary with human summary because the computing process is different from human thinking processes.
2. Develop an intelligent summarization system that can make a human-level summarization. Jim Gray proposed the challenge of expert-level summarization in his Turing lecture in 2003. Solving this problem requires an intelligent summarization system to have the same level of knowledge, information modelling ability and cognitive ability as human experts. It is hard to reach this goal by just improving the traditional computing process. Figure 1.11 depicts the way to realize human-level summarization by simulating human knowledge.

The following essential questions are critical for transforming the paradigm of summarization research [142]:

1. What is summarization, whether the best summary of a given representation exists or not?
2. What are the fundamental principles and rules of language use and understanding behind summarization? Can the principles and rules be applied to improve summarization? In-depth research on summarization can deepen the understanding of language use and understanding.

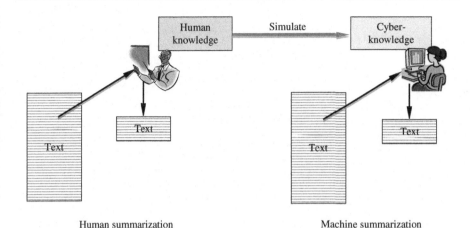

Figure 1.11 Realizing human-level summarization by simulating human knowledge.

3. What is the appropriate research methodology for studying summarization and developing summarization systems?
4. Can we find a general summarization method?

The following sections are concerned with the following points:

1. Regarding text summarization as a special case of investigating the general summarization methodology.
2. Regarding things (text as an instance) as a near decomposable system that emerges patterns with certain rules.
3. Regarding things to be summarised, human (including the behaviours of reading, understanding and writing), and summarization system as the components of an unified research object, investigating the interactions between them and relevant rules from different scales and dimensions, and understanding the influence on summarization.
4. Obtaining inspiration from other disciplines such as linguistics, cognitive science and psychology as different dimensions to carry out fundamental exploration in a multiple dimensional methodology space.

The emerging structures

2

A complex system often consists of components that weakly interact with each other but are not negligible. Simon named such a system near decomposable system and proposed the propositions of near decomposability, which interprets the behaviors of many complex systems. The underlying assumption is that all observers share a unified cognition paradigm: bottom-up aggregation. This chapter extends the research object to a dual system consisting of the observed complex system and the memory of the system, proposes new propositions considering the integrity of representation and a semantic emerging structure, verifies the propositions and the emerging rules through text summarization, and proposes new principles regarding text as a near decomposable system. The structure of text emerges with representing components independently and linking components with rules. The study of emerging near decomposable structure provides a new way to understand text, summarization and the near decomposability.

2.1 Near decomposability

For an organization, there are generally more interactions among the employees of the same department than among the employees of different departments. Such a complex system has a hierarchical structure. A hierarchical system is called a near decomposable system when the intra-component linkages are generally stronger than the inter-component linkages.

H. A. Simon, a Nobel Prize laureate, gave the following two propositions about the near decomposable systems [110]:

1. *The short-term behaviors of each of the subsystems are approximately independent of the short-term behaviors of the other subsystems.*
2. *The behaviors of anyone of the subsystems depend on the behaviors of the other subsystems in only an aggregate way in the long-term.*

A near decomposable system separates the high-frequency dynamics of the interactions within the internal structure of the subsystems from the low-frequency dynamics of the interactions among subsystems. Only the aggregative properties of the subsystems participate in the interactions of the subsystems. The above two propositions can interpret the structure of many complex systems like social networks.

A complex system may be evolved from an empty world: *most things are only weakly linked to most other things, and only a tiny part of all possible interactions needs to be considered for a tolerable description of the reality.* This assumption provides the rationale for designing an iterative process to simulate the emerging structure of a near decomposable system.

Multi-Dimensional Summarization in Cyber-Physical Society. DOI: http://dx.doi.org/10.1016/B978-0-12-803455-2.00002-0

The underlying assumption is that all complex systems share the same way of construction and all observers of the complex system share a unified cognition paradigm: bottom-up aggregation.

The following sections will extend the research object to a dual system consisting of the observed complex system and the memory of the system, propose new propositions considering the integrity of representation and a semantic emerging structure, verify the propositions and the emerging rules through text summarization, and propose new principles regarding text as a near decomposable system.

2.2   Text as near decomposable system

A normal text such as book and paper can be regarded as a near decomposable system because of the following facts:

1. A text can be decomposed into paragraphs or sections that can be further decomposed into paragraphs or sections (subsections) in structure.
2. Sentences are more closely related within paragraphs than between paragraphs as sentences within one paragraph render one theme.
3. Paragraphs are more closely related within sections than between sections as paragraphs within one section render one theme.
4. The short-term behaviors such as writing and reading one component (sentence, paragraph, section, etc.) are approximately independent of the short-term behaviors on the other components although the definitions of the short-term are different with regard to different scales. All components are connected in an aggregate way to contribute to the formation of the structure of a larger component (paragraph, section, or text).

Scientific paper is a near decomposable system since it consists of sections, each section consists of paragraphs or sections (subsections), and each paragraph consists of sentences. The short-term behaviors (writing and reading) on each section (paragraph or sentence) are approximately independent of the short-term behaviors on the other section (paragraph or sentence). All sections are linked to contribute to the formation of the paper, all paragraphs are linked to contribute to the formation of the section they belong to, and all sentences are linked to contribute to the formation of the paragraph they belong to.

Scientific book is a typical near decomposable system that contains one more level, chapter, compared with the hierarchical structure of paper. Scientific area is a near decomposable system since it consists of papers and books that were written by different researchers independently. The short-term behaviors (reading and writing) on one paper or book are independent from the short-term behaviors on the other papers or books, and all papers and books of the area are linked through citation to contribute to the formation and evolution of the area.

Simon's propositions provide an interpretation for many complex systems. The assumption of bottom-up aggregation guides people to observe and construct a complex system. The two propositions have the following issues:

1. There are no formal definitions of short-term and long-term, short-term behavior and long-term behavior, as well as dependency and independency. It can be taken for granted that the behavior of writing or scanning a sentence is independent of the behavior of writing or scanning the other sentences, but the long-term behaviors on sentences are no longer writing or scanning. The long-term behaviors will be memorizing and understanding behaviours. There is a huge gap between scanning text and understanding text.
2. The behaviors of components are connected in only an aggregate way. This excludes other ways of connection. The understanding of one sentence is not only relevant to the understanding of the other sentences within the paragraph but also the understanding of the sentences within other paragraphs.
3. It is more suitable for guiding the construction of a complex system than analyzing a complex system because analysis involves understanding and insight, which varies with the knowledge of analyzers.
4. A complex system is viewed from one dimension. Two components viewed from one dimension may be viewed as one component from another dimension, and one component viewed from one dimension may be viewed as two components from another dimension. For example, two paragraphs distributed at different locations within a text may render the same theme.

2.3   The near decomposability of memory

Observing or operating a complex system leaves images in memories. A basic experience from self-observation is that separately memorizing the components (e.g., arms and legs) of a thing (e.g., body) does not take priority when the whole can be observed directly. In other words, a feature of human memorization is that things tend to be remembered as integral. This integrity sets a constraint for the proposition of the independency of the short-term behaviors of the complex system.

Independency of short-term memory: *The integral short-term memory of any component is approximately independent of the integral short-term memory of the other components.*

This indicates that different components are formed and understood relatively independent of each other in short-term for the integrity of behaviors. A general artificial system concerns structure and function (transforming input into output). A meaningful natural language representation concerns the structure of text, the structure of memory and understanding, which relies on humans—writers and readers.

In the long-term memory, the minds link the memories of the current components to the memories of the existing components, accept the new memories, and carry out reasoning that may generate new links. The ability of rendering meaning by linking memories is the basis of imagination. The memories of all components contribute to the memory of the whole representation. The following proposition extends the Simon's proposition from the "only aggregate way" to various semantic links, such as the is-part-of link, the cause-effect link and the sequential link.

Long-term emerge: *The memory of any one of the components depends on the memories of the other components through some semantic links in the long-term.*

The above two new propositions indicate that the structure of text emerges with independent short-term memories of components and linking memories in the long-term memory. The memory emerges the structure of the observed system and mediates understanding.

2.4   The structure emerging through representing and understanding

Different from the static models that identify the features of objects (word frequency) in representation, the process of representation reflects the means for generating objects with the expected characteristics. Viewing text as a process of representing and understanding helps unveil the principles and rules of representing and understanding text.

Let us observe how a structure emerges with writing sentence by sentence as shown in Figure 2.1. The appropriate words were selected to cooperatively contribute to the formation of the first sentence. The first sentence contributes to the selection of words for writing the second sentence. The second sentence contributes to

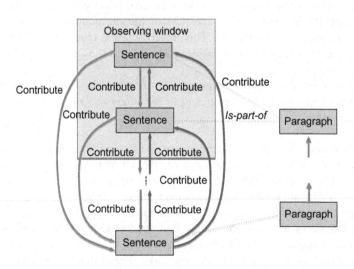

Figure 2.1 The process of emerging the structure of text.

complete, interpret, or extend the first sentence. The first sentence and the second sentence contribute to the selection of the appropriate words for writing the third sentence (the second sentence may have more contribution due to the fresh memory). The latter sentence contributes to complete, explain or extend the former sentences to render a richer content, and contributes to the selection of the appropriate words for writing the following sentences. A window of all former sentences provides the context for writing or reading the current sentence, and the current sentence completes, interprets or extends the former sentences. The size of the window depends on individuals and on the scale of the text for writing or reading. The language representation components of different scales such as sentence, paragraph, and section provide different scales and levels of representation through the "contribute" link.

In addition to the *contribute* link, the *co-occurrence* of words further links the current sentence to the former sentences, and there are some other links such as *cause-effect, generalization-of, specialization-of* and *instance-of* between sentences. All of the semantic links connect sentences to render a kind of semantic structure of the paragraphs, which further link one another to contribute to rendering the semantic structure of the text. The emerging structure records the basic behaviors of forming the state (language representation structure) and the processes of memorizing and understanding while writing and reading.

Some rules enable the language representation components of different granularities to render the structure with different contributions to form the larger representation components. The contributions of different components reinforce one another when rendering the structure of the language representation and the semantic structure.

Scientific papers have two characteristics: *structured* and *explicit citation*. The explicit citation connects papers to form the structures of research areas. The semantic links form the implicit citations that render the semantic structure. Modeling the formation of the structure is a way to make summarization based on the structure information.

A way to text summarization is to rank nodes, select high-rank nodes, and then compose them. However, previous graph ranking methods reflect the degree of connections, which has little semantics. The basic assumption of semantic links is that it is hard to accurately represent the semantics of text, and a semantic link network of components such as words, sentences, paragraphs, and sections can render more semantics of the system than a general graph [139,141].

2.5   Principles for emerging sentences within text

The basic assumption of text summarization is that some representation components (e.g., sentences) of text contribute more than the others in rendering its semantic structure because a summary is limited in capacity to contain all components in the original text. The components selected in the summary are regarded as more important than others in making contribution to render the semantics (from the summarizer's point of view). With this assumption, the key issue of extractive summarization is how to differentiate the contribution of different components to the component they commonly belong to, e.g., the contribution of different sentences to paragraphs and sections.

From the value point of view, parts contribute values to the whole. The key is the way to measure the value. In Marxian economics, the value of a product is measured by the value of the labor that produces the product. This indicates the following principle for measuring sentences, which can be used for extractive summarization:

Principles for measuring sentences: *The measure of sentence is effective only when the following conditions are satisfied*:

1. *The measure can apply to the larger components of representation such as paragraph and section that contribute to emerging the structure of the text.*
2. *The measure satisfies the additivity of an effective value chain, i.e., the linear combination of the measures of parts is not more than the measure of the whole.*

In other words, the measure is rational only when it can uniformly measure the components of different scales that jointly contribute to emerge the structure of the text as a complex system. Based on this principle, an extractive summarization mechanism can be developed by ranking and selecting sentences.

The scientific goal of research ensures that any scientific paper has at least one core. All representation components of smaller granularity contribute to emerge the cores of the representation components of larger granularities they belong to. One component can contribute to multiple components. As an effect of contribution propagation, multiple cores of a paper may emerge. In this case, the small representation components contribute more evenly to different cores.

2.6   Rules for emerging structure within text

The hierarchical structure of text concerns some basic rules between parts and the whole:

1. Every representation component is a part of itself.
2. A part of a part of a whole is itself a part of that whole, i.e., A is a part of C if A is a part of B and B is a part of C. For example, a word is a part of sentence, which is a part of paragraph, so a word is a part of the paragraph that contains the word.
3. Two different parts cannot be a part of the other, i.e., A cannot be a part of B if they are different. For example, two different sentences cannot be a part of each other. This also implies that A cannot be a part of B if B is a part of A.

It is necessary to assume that the text to be summarized has basic quality, and the readers and writers largely have the same cognitive level.

Basic assumption: *Writers of the discussed texts have wisdom in expressing ideas with a certain aim and in a coherent way. Readers are at the same cognitive level as the writers.*

The interactions between parts as well as between parts and the whole emerge the structure of text according to the assumption of coherence between the neighbor representations of different scales. Comparing with other decomposable systems, text has a distinguished characteristic: the basic components—words—have strong links between larger components (sentences, paragraphs, sections, etc.) to render the semantics of different scales. The coherence assumption indicates the following rule, which interprets how one sentence influences another sentence within text.

Rule 1: *The contribution from a sentence to the neighbor sentence in completing, interpreting or extending meaning is determined by the relations between the words of the two sentences.*

The basic assumption assumes that any representation component within text is not isolated. The contribution of a representation component to the larger representation component depends on the contribution from its internal components and the external components. The following rules are on three types of representation units: sentence, paragraph and section.

Rule 2: *The contribution from a sentence to its paragraph is determined by the contributions from its words and the contributions from its neighbor sentences.*

Rule 3: *The contribution from a paragraph to its section is determined by the contributions from its sentences and the contribution from the neighbor paragraphs.*

Rule 4: *The contribution from a section to the paper is determined by the contributions from its paragraphs and the contribution from the neighbor sections.*

The sentence, the paragraph and the section that contain a word provide the contexts of different granularities for the word, and they jointly enforce the contribution of the word.

Rule 5: *The contribution from a word to a sentence is determined by the contribution (to the paragraph) from the sentence that contains the word, by the contribution (to the section) from the paragraphs that contain the word, and by the contribution (to the paper) from the sections that contains the word.*

One word can contribute to different sentences within the same paragraph or multiple paragraphs within the text. The following rule is for measuring the contribution.

Rule 6: *The contribution from component X to component Y that includes X is proportional to the contribution from Y to the component Z that includes Y.*

The above rules imply a function that transforms the contributions, so the iterative computing models on the *is-part-of* semantic link network can be further designed to model the structure of a paper. Figure 2.2 depicts the reciprocal relations between words, sentences, paragraphs, sections and papers. The solid black line denotes the *is-part-of* relation, the blue arrows denote contribution, the red arrows denote the reaction of the contribution, and the dotted black arrows denote citation between papers. Citation links connect papers to render the *is-part-of* relation to form a research area.

The following section is to verify the above propositions and emerging rules in the application scenario of text summarization.

2.7   Case study: summarizing text with emerging structure

This section will take text summarization as an application to verify the role of relations in rendering components for text summarization.

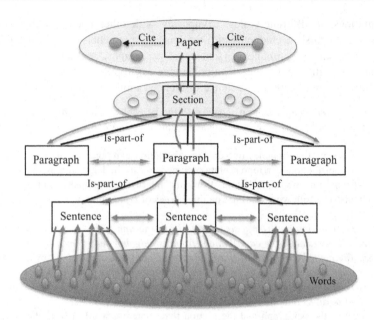

Figure 2.2 Reciprocal relations between words, sentences, paragraphs, sections and papers.

The *is-part-of* relation is the basic relation that forms a near decomposable system, so the first stage of this study focuses on the *is-part-of* relation within a single scientific paper. The *is-part-of* relation organizes words within sentences, organizes sentences within paragraphs, organizes paragraphs within sections, and organizes sections within a paper. Different representation components have different contributions to the process of emerging the whole structure. The differences between representation components emerge the structure for making summarization.

The process of emerging contributions from the components of different scales can be simulated through an iterative function. Therefore, the sentences with higher contributions can be selected for making summarization. The advantages of using the emerging structure for text summarization will be assessed by both the objective data and the subjective human observation.

2.7.1 Iterative function

To compute the weight vector of sentences, an iterative function $w = f(w, s, p, c)$ is used to approximately compute the word-weight vector w through an iterative process. The sentence-weight vector s, the paragraph-weight vector p, and the section-weight vector c can be then directly computed based on the word-weight vector through summing parts according to the *is-part-of* relation.

The matrix multiplication is used to represent the weight summation relation between weigh vectors of different nodes through the adjacent matrix. An adjacent matrix W_S is used to represent word-sentence connections (the row is word ID in word vector w and the column is sentence ID in weight vector s). The S_P matrix is for the sentence-paragraph connections and P_C for paragraph-section connections.

Formula (2.1) represents that the sentence-weight vector s is the summation of the weights of the words it contains. The sentence-paragraph weight relation is represented by formula (2.2). The formula (2.3) represents the paragraph-section relation. Finally, the weight of word is the summation of the weights of sentences, paragraphs and sections where it is located in, which is determined by the matrix multiplication of the corresponding adjacent matrices W_S, S_P, and P_C in formula (2.4). The weight vectors in the right-hand side of the formulas are normalized.

$$s^{(n)} = W_S \times w^{(n)} \tag{2.1}$$

$$p^{(n)} = S_P^T \times s^{(n)} \tag{2.2}$$

$$c^{(n)} = P_C^T \times p^{(n)} \tag{2.3}$$

$$w^{(n+1)} = W_S \times S^{(n)} + W_S \times S_P \times p^{(n)} + W_S \times S_P \times P_C \times c^{(n)} \tag{2.4}$$

Replacing the three weight vector variables of the right-hand side of Eq. (2.4) with those defined in Eqs. (2.1), (2.2) and (2.3) obtains an iterative function defined on the word weight vector:

$$w^{(n+1)} = (W_S \times W_S^T + W_S \times S_P \times S_P^T \times W_S^T + W_S \times S_P \times P_C \times P_C^T \times S_P^T \times W_S^T) \times w^{(n)} \tag{2.5}$$

Let $A = W_S \times W_S^T + W_S \times S_P \times S_P^T \times W_S^T + W_S \times S_P \times P_C \times P_C^T \times S_P^T \times W_S^T,$ $\quad$ (2.6)

Finally, an iterative function formula (2.7) over the word weight vector w is obtained:

$$w^{(n+1)} = Aw. \tag{2.7}$$

For different structures, those relation formulas can be manipulated by either adding more relations to the structure or eliminating some relations from the structure. For example, if there is no section node in the graph, formula (2.3) and the corresponding term in formula (2.4) can be removed to form an iterative function consisting of words, sentences and paragraphs.

More complicated relations can be incorporated into the structure. A sentence distance can be used to measure the similarity between two sentences. The TextRank model used the sentence similarity distance to build a graph for ranking sentences by the PageRank algorithm. Intuitively, if many sentences are quite similar to one sentence, this sentence is likely to be an important sentence to make more contribution to the paper. Sentence similarity reflects a global semantic distribution but it does not consider the structure of a document. To combine this sentence similarity with the structure of the paper, formula (2.1) is modified by adding a weight vector of sentences that is computed from the sentence distance matrix. A sentence-to-sentence distance matrix S_S can be obtained firstly by computing the Jaccard distance of sentence pairs within a paper. Then, a PageRank weight vector s_p using S_S can be obtained. Formula (2.8) is the computing model of the PageRank algorithm, where α is empirically set as 0.85 and the dangling node vector p_d is set as $1/n$. That is, for those sink nodes, we just randomly set up an out link to other nodes. Finally, s_p is integrated into formula (2.9) with the weight vector s from the structural graph computing process using weight factors β_1 and β_2. We set β_1 and β_2 to 0.5, that is, the final weight of a sentence is determined by the sentence similarity information and the structural information, and the rest of formulas remain the same.

$$s_p^{(n+1)} = \alpha S_S \times s_p^{(n+1)} + (1 - \alpha) \times p_d. \tag{2.8}$$

$$s^{(n+1)} = \beta_1 s_p^{(n+1)} + \beta_2 W s \times s^{(n)}. \tag{2.9}$$

2.7.2 Experiment

The experiment starts with extracting 175 scientific papers in the proceedings of ACL2014 from the ACL Anthology (https://aclweb.org/anthology/P/P14/) as the benchmark test set. The abstracts and conclusions of the papers are extracted as the gold standard for the single-paper summarization. The basic assumption is that the abstract and conclusion are the best components that render the theme of a paper. The result of the extractive summarization is evaluated by comparing the extracted sentences with the sentences in the abstract and conclusion.

Two types of tests are conducted and prepared: (1) In the inclusion-test benchmark (Include-Test in simple), the text includes abstract and conclusion. A text summarization system can extract sentences from the abstract and the conclusion. (2) In the exclusion-test benchmark (Exclude-Test), texts in abstract and conclusion are removed from the text. Therefore, it is impossible for a summarization system to extract sentences from the abstract and the conclusion.

DUC2002 benchmark data is used to evaluate the structure model on those short texts that have no obvious human-labeled structures (http://www-nlpir.nist.gov/projects/duc/guidelines/2002.html). DUC2002 benchmark data set contains a set of short news document texts and human-labeled summarization benchmark for evaluating summarization models.

The experiments on the following cases are compared to show how the structure information can improve the quality of extractive summarization. The following are possible structures:

- Para: The structure contains words, sentences and paragraphs.
- SubPara: The structure contains words, sentences, sub-paragraphs and paragraphs.
- Section: The structure contains words, sentences, paragraphs and sections.

- Section + Title: The structure contains words, sentences, paragraphs and sections. Keywords from section titles are extracted to build another semantic link network to emphasize those keywords in the titles of sections.
- SecSub: The structure contains words, sentences, sub-paragraphs, paragraphs and sections.
- GS + SubPara: Combing the relation based on sentence similarity with the structure in the SubPara mode.

The above structure is compared with other classical models that did not use the structure information within the paper.

- TF-IDF: Ranking each sentence within the paper, each sentence is treated as one document, and the TF-IDF matrix is computed from the sentence set of the paper. A weight vector of sentences is computed by summing the TF-IDF weights of words in that sentence.
- GS: A semantic link network consisting of sentences as nodes and the similarity between sentences as links. PageRank algorithm is applied to the network to derive the weight of each sentence. The GS model is an implementation of TextRank [79].
- GW: A semantic link network consisting of words as nodes and links as the relations between the words of the same sentence within a given window. The weight of each word is obtained by applying the PageRank algorithm over the semantic link network. The weight of each sentence is the summation of the weights of words within that sentence.

ROUGE is a widely used tool for automatically evaluating the summarization quality by comparing the summarization text with the golden standard benchmark [63]. It is used to evaluate the summarization quality. ROUGE-N is a standard metric for the DUC competition. The basic idea of ROUGE-N is to evaluate the overlapping parts between the generated summary and the standard summary in N-gram unit. ROUGE-N is computed below:

$$\text{ROUGE} - \text{N} = \frac{\sum_{S \in B} \sum_{\text{ngram} \in G} \text{Count}_{\text{match}}(\text{ngram})}{\sum_{S \in B} \sum_{\text{ngram} \in G} \text{Count}(\text{ngram})}$$

Where $\text{Count}_{\text{match}}$ (ngram) is the maximal number of co-occurrence of N-grams in both the generated sentence set and the benchmark summary, and Count(ngram) is the number of N-grams in the benchmark. ROUGE-1 is one such metric that is close to human evaluation [64]. ROUGE-N score has been widely used to compare summarization models on the public benchmark data set in which standard summarization are given for evaluating the summary.

2.7.3 Experiment result

Table 2.1 and 2.2 show the ROUGE scores (at the 95% confidence interval) of the Include-Test and Exclude-Test. The recall rate of ROUGE-1, ROUGE-2, ROUGE-3, ROUGE-4 and ROUGE-L metrics is listed. In all test, the GS + SubPara model achieved the best score. The GS model has better ROUGE-1 score than the SubPara model in the Exclude-Test. In the Include-Test, the proposed

Table 2.1 **Rouge score of Include-Test**

	ROUGE-1	ROUGE-2	ROUGE-3	ROUGE-4	ROUGE-L
GW	0.23156	0.03410	0.01541	0.01174	0.21492
TFIDF	0.40974	0.15243	0.10622	0.09207	0.36365
GS	0.42379	0.14418	0.08612	0.06868	0.38109
Para	0.40941	0.15031	0.09561	0.07801	0.37182
SubPara	0.44308	0.20257	0.14955	0.13063	0.40790
Section	0.41827	0.15977	0.10483	0.08734	0.38082
Section + Tiltle	0.40127	0.12697	0.10254	0.07714	0.34012
SecSub	0.42547	0.17521	0.12086	0.10279	0.38890
GS + SubPara	**0.45884**	**0.20843**	**0.15102**	**0.13072**	**0.42118**

Table 2.2 **Rouge score of Exclude-Test**

	ROUGE-1	ROUGE-2	ROUGE-3	ROUGE-4	ROUGE-L
GW	0.22521	0.02294	0.00427	0.00158	0.20829
TFIDF	0.36167	0.07670	0.02667	0.01275	0.30869
GS	0.38275	0.08726	0.02845	0.01288	0.33828
Para	0.37754	0.09558	0.03595	0.01766	0.33525
SubPara	0.37664	0.09472	0.03452	0.01699	0.33435
Section	0.37084	0.09006	0.03238	0.01637	0.32960
Section + Tiltle	0.36095	0.08116	0.03318	0.01612	0.31260
SecSub	0.37490	0.09388	0.03528	0.01792	0.33343
GS + SubPara	**0.39140**	**0.10256**	**0.03853**	**0.01916**	**0.34671**

SubPara and GS + SubPara models achieved a significant improvement over other models including the GS model. All models have a better score in the Include-Test than in the Exclude-Test because in the Include-Test the abstract and conclusion text are also included in the summarization process. The Section + Title model does not make improvement over the Section model because the titles of the sections of a paper often use much more general words that may not directly reflect the contents of the work. Emphasizing on those keywords will make the results biased to those words that do not significantly contribute to emerge the structure of the paper.

Table 2.3 shows the ROUGE scores (at the 95% confidence interval) of the tests on the DUC2002 data set. As DUC2002 texts have no sections, the experiment does not verify the texts that have sections. The GS + SubPara model also achieved the best score in this test.

2.7.4 Discussion

The GS + SubPara model incorporates a typical link (similar relation based on word co-occurrence) into the semantic link network within a paper, which can be deemed as a hybrid graph containing two types of links, one is *is-part-of*, which

Table 2.3 **Rouge score of DUC-Test**

	ROUGE-1	ROUGE-2	ROUGE-3	ROUGE-4	ROUGE-L
GW	0.40547	0.14107	0.08549	0.06167	0.37757
TFIDF	0.47545	0.19936	0.12612	0.09259	0.43567
GS	0.48967	0.20647	0.12800	0.09250	0.45185
Para	0.48759	0.21612	0.13758	0.10036	0.45259
SubPara	0.48597	0.21540	0.13769	0.10077	0.45131
GS + SubPara	**0.49714**	**0.22259**	**0.14227**	**0.10408**	**0.46062**

Table 2.4 **Rouge score improvement of GS + SubPara model**

Test type	Gains of model	ROUGE-1	ROUGE-2	ROUGE-3	ROUGE-4	ROUGE-L
Include-Test	Gain on GS	0.03505	0.06425	0.0649	0.06204	0.04009
	Gain on SubPara	0.01576	0.00586	0.00147	0.00009	0.01328
Exclude-Test	Gain on GS	0.00865	0.0153	0.01008	0.00628	0.00843
	Gain on SubPara	0.01476	0.00784	0.00401	0.00217	0.01236
DUC-Test	Gain on GS	0.00747	0.01612	0.01427	0.01158	0.00877
	Gain on SubPara	0.01117	0.00719	0.00458	0.00331	0.00931

renders the structure of a paper, and the other is *is-similar-to*, which renders the similarity between two sentences. The similar link covers the whole range of a paper. Any two sentences within a paper can be related as long as there is a common word in two sentences. In the structure graph, two sentences are related when they are in the same paragraph or section or they have a common word. However, there is no direct link to represent the similarity between two sentences, and the similarity measure cannot be reflected by this indirect link between two sentences through the *is-part-of* link between sentence and word.

When using the structure based on the similarity between sentences, each sentence will have three types of links: the similar-to links to the other sentences, the *is-part-of* links to its paragraph node, and the *is-part-of* link from its words.

The experiment result shows that incorporating the link between sentences based on common words into the approach used in the first phase can improve the result. Table 2.4 shows that the GS + SubPara get improvements on ROUGE score compared with the GS model and the SubPara model respectively in three experiments. One can see that GS + SubPara gets less improvement in the DUC-Test whose texts have less structure and shorter length. In the Include-Test, an improvement of more than 1% is achieved. This also shows that different links play similar role in rendering the theme of a paper.

Although the summarization result cannot compete with human-level summarization, the high-rank sentences are indeed important sentences. Figure 2.3 shows the sentences extracted from the paper [143] by the GS model and the GS + SubPara model. To compare the quality of the summarization sentences, colors are used to show the relatedness of an extracted sentence to the original sentence within the author's abstract text.

Figure 2.4 lists three sentences in different colors selected from the abstract, which reflect the three major ideas discussed in the paper. If an extracted sentence is related to one of the three sentences, they will be colored the same, and assigned

The GS model:3.5/15	The GS+SubPara model:5/13
1. It is important to ensure the understandability and expressiveness of the integrated representation.	1. e) Construct a semantic link network of pictures, tags and language representations in relevant texts as the summary.
2. From this point of view, summarization can be regarded as a transformation of reducing the dimensions of a representation so that the dimensions of representation can be linked to and merge with the dimensions in the mental space. 0.5	2. A summarization system consisting of a multi-dimensional classification space of summary in form of semantic link network of pictures and language representations and a requirement space defined and managed by users. 1
3. The suitable summarizer for summarizing a representation is rendered by the social network of its writers and readers.	3. The form of summary can be a semantic link network of texts, pictures, audios, and videos.
4. 5) The representation of knowledge is not unique, and the understanding of representation is not unique.	4. One semantic link network of texts can link to the other semantic link networks of texts to form a larger semantic link network through such relations as citation and coauthor. 0.5
5. The semantic link network can be regarded as the map of the cyberspace and social space.	5. The union of the semantic link network and the classification space forms a complex classification space used to represent and organize semantic images.
6. The reasonable method is to study the multiple dimensions of the summarization environment and to consider the reasonable result.	6. summary should use the core representations in the original representation. 1
7. Citations form the intention and extension of a representation. 1	7. The intention of representation is indicated by core representations and by citation from other representations. 0.5
8. The union of the semantic link network and the classification space forms a complex classification space used to represent and organize semantic images.	8. The representation that has a direct link to the core representation is close-core representation. 1
9. It is necessary to review previous efforts and explore the foundation of summarization.	9. A solution is to establish the semantic links between pictures, discover the communities of the semantic link network of pictures, select one picture to represent one community, and construct a network of the representative pictures.
10. Exploring citation is a way to explore the nature of summarization. 1	10. A semantic link network of important concepts and relations can help readers quickly know the main cues and measures in representations.
11. Construct a semantic link network of pictures, tags and language representations in relevant texts as the summary.	11. The core representation renders the core idea of a representation. 1
12. The knowledge provides the rules of representation and understanding.	12. Figure 8 depicts the idea of constructing a semantic link network of pictures and tags as a summary.
13. The basic characteristics and principles of language use and understanding indicate the following dimensions for evaluating a summarization.	13. The semantic link network can be regarded as the map of the cyberspace and social space.
14. One semantic link network of texts can link to the other semantic link networks of texts to form a larger semantic link network through such relations as citation and coauthor. 1	
15. Figure 8 depicts the idea of constructing a semantic link network of pictures and tags as a summary.	

Figure 2.3 Summarizing the paper [143] by extracting sentences using the GS and the GS + SubPara model.

"*The basic viewpoints include:*
(1) a representation suitable for summarization should have a core, indicated by its intention and extension;
(2) summarization is an open process of various interactions, involved in various explicit and implicit citations;
(3) *and,the form of summary is diverse and summarization carries out through multiple dimensions.*"

Figure 2.4 Last three sentences in the abstract of the paper [143].

a score by a group of invited readers (1 for directly related, 0.5 for indirectly related, and 0 for unrelated). As shown in Figure 2.3, the result of GS + SubPara is obviously better than the GS model in both the topic coverage and the relatedness to the three sentences in the abstract.

2.8 Emerging structure through dimensions

It is hard to accurately identify which component takes priority to emerge by measuring and comparing the importance between components because some factors are objective and some are subjective. The frequency of words and the *is-part-of* relation are objective while the contribution or importance is more subjective, to writers and readers.

A set of representations like sentences can be viewed from different dimensions (the following chapters will look into the dimension in detail, here a dimension can be understood as the dimension in the distance space). Different structures will emerge along different dimensions. Figure 2.5 depicts a three-dimensional space where representations can be compared from different dimensions. The distance between two representations in the multi-dimensional space can be defined according to the distance between their projections onto different dimensions.

The following are the interpretation of the two dimensions: *Intensity* and *cost*.

1. *Intensity (of link)*. A sentence can be regarded as a node of a semantic link network of sentences. As the total number of words people often used is limited, a sentence containing more words has a higher probability to link to more other sentences by sharing the words, by connecting words, or by contributing words to the same sentence; for example, the sentence containing words w_1, w_2, and w_3 and the sentence containing words w_4, w_5, and w_6 contribute w_3 and w_4 respectively to the sentence that contains words w_3 and w_4.
2. *Cost*. A writer using more words to express the meaning of a sentence spends more manpower and time, which represents certain intensity, based on the basic assumption of writer and reader. A sentence with more words costs more energy of writing. On the other hand, a reader needs to spend more time to read a sentence that contains more words and has a higher probability to spend more time to understand it. This is in line with the cognitive economic principle [22].

Representations can be compared by projecting them onto different dimensions of the space. For a particular system, some dimensions play the key role but others are

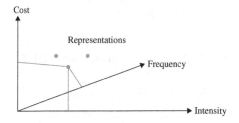

Figure 2.5 Emerge structure through dimensions.

not negligible. For example, projecting sentences onto the intensity of link dimension and the cost dimension can get the following interpretation of emerging: *A sentence that contains more number of words than another sentence within the same paragraph takes a higher probability to emerge in contributing to the formation of the paragraph.*

If all sentences within a text contain largely the same number of words, the number of sentences plays an important role within a paragraph. A set of paragraphs can be also viewed from the following two dimensions.

1. *Intensity (of link).* A paragraph can be regarded as a community on the semantic link network of sentences. Sentences within the paragraph are more tightly connected to render a topic than the sentences between paragraphs. On one hand, a paragraph containing richer semantic links indicates higher intensity of link. On the other hand, a paragraph that contains more sentences has a high probability to share more words between paragraphs, to contain more connection words, and to contribute to more common sentences. A paragraph is also a node of the semantic link network of paragraphs. A paragraph that contains more sentences has a higher probability to establish richer semantic links to more number of paragraphs, for example, by sharing words in sentences or establishing semantic links (e.g., similar, cause-effect,etc.) between sentences.

2. *Cost.* A paragraph containing more sentences spends more manpower and time than the paragraph that contains less number of sentences. It is more economic to use less number of sentences to express the same meaning. On the other hand, a reader needs to spend more time to read a paragraph that contains more sentences and has a higher probability to spend more time to understand it due to the shift of patterns in different sentences. On the other hand, a paragraph containing more sentences occupies the higher percentage of mass in the network. For example, a community that contains 30 nodes occupies higher percentage of the total mass than the community that contains 10 nodes within the same network.

The views from the above two dimensions indicate the following interpretation of emerging: *A paragraph that contains richer links and more sentences than other paragraphs within the same section takes a higher probability to emerge to make contribution to the formation of the section.*

Similar interpretation applies to section and applies to research paper, topic and area. However, more does not always mean better, just as the term frequency measure for information retrieval. Mapping representations into other dimensions can get other interpretations. *A full interpretation is the summarization of the interpretations at different dimensions.*

Chapter 4, The semantic lens and Chapter 5, Multi-dimensional methodology, will discuss the multi-dimensional space in detail.

2.9 Emerging from psychological dimension

2.9.1 Assumptions of reading

The question of what makes a statement "important" in a story was studied [116]. The following two criteria were found to predict the judgments of importance: (1) The number of direct causal links, and (2) whether or not an event was in a causal chain from the opening to the closing of the story. The importance of a statement increases with the number of causal links and causal chain membership. Causal link is one type of semantic link. Research in psychology provides an evidence for the richness definition of the semantic link network [140], and gives an interpretation for the rules of emerging structure.

Psychologists proposed the following three assumptions [45,46]:

1. Goal assumption, that is, a reader is to reach a goal through reading.
2. Coherence assumption. Local coherence is established when a reading representation is linked to the existing concept in the short-term memory. Global coherence is established when a reading representation (i.e., sentence) is linked to the existing concepts of the previous reading representations in the long-term memory. The coherence assumption explains the integrity constraint introduced in Section 2.3.
3. Interpretation assumption. Readers will try to interpret the cause of events, behaviors and states. Reading is mainly driven by generating and answering questions.

The above assumptions provide a psychological dimension for assessing the importance of a representation. The "importance" is from the author's point of view at this dimension. Sometimes goals may not be predetermined and may be built during reading process. Goals can be strong or weak in different cases. Coherence can be at the high abstraction level besides the word level and the basic concept level, and coherence can be indirect (e.g., word A and word B can be coherent as follows: A is mapped into concept C and B is mapped into concept C', and there is a implicit link between C and C'). Different types of semantic links have different extents of coherence. The cause-effect link between concepts is a strong coherence. Interpretation is necessary but it can be either a strong interpretation or a weak interpretation in different cases. Measuring the priority of emerging a representation needs to consider the distance between the representation and the goal, the cause-effect link, and the question in a multi-dimensional space.

2.9.2 Interactive environment

Different from traditional text environments, an interactive environment such as Whatsapp and Wechat has the following characteristics:

1. A text rendering an integral theme is formed through an interaction process.
2. Both readers and writers participate in the same interaction process.
3. Each writer contributes a short representation such as a sentence and a picture.

The following are assumptions for an interactive environment:

1. *Dynamic goal.* A conversation may start from a question or just a message without a clear goal, while the goal can be inspired or formed through an interaction process. The initial sentence or a picture may be developed into an idea consisting of a series of short representations such as sentences, pictures or links.
2. *Dynamic coherence.* Coherence mainly keeps within a window of conversation, which changes in size to reflect the current interest. As interest can change quickly, global coherence in conversation history makes little sense because of the forget effect and the

new interests generated. The windows in the conversation history provide a certain context for the understanding of the current conversation. For example, a newcomer may not understand some conversations. Global coherence exists within the semantic link network of concepts in the individuals' mental spaces when representations (i.e., sentences and images) are mapped into the existing concepts in the long-term memory. The semantic link network of concepts provides a global context for understanding the current conversation. The local context, the global context and the contents provided by individuals constitute a three-tier context, which can help understand the conversation and recommend appropriate words and phrases to speed up users' inputs for effective discussion.

3. *Query-based interpretation.* Readers tend to ask questions when they have problems rather than making an effort to find the answers by themselves. Writers have the sense of quickly answering questions in short term. Query-answer happens often within a conversation window. Conversation mainly develops with generating and answering questions. Semantic links, especially the casual link, plays an important role in seeking answers.

4. *Interest-led extension.* Participants tend to extend the previous representations (sentences or pictures) to construct an integral meaning. Semantic links, especially the casual link, can arouse interests. The current interest will quickly phase out when a new interest is generated.

The whole conversation history constitutes a near decomposable system, in which components are the windows on the particular themes or the composition of the windows on the same theme. The near decomposable system evolves with the development of the conversation.

Summarizing the conversation windows on the same theme in the conversation history enables participants to know the context quickly. A function can be added to the conversation interface by which the participants can click to display the summary of the theme.

2.10   The cognitive level of current text summarization

Summarization is a process of representation. Current research uses the existing summarization results or human summarization results as the criteria to evaluate new summarizations. What is the cognitive level of a summarization? What is the reference frame for determining the cognitive level?

An original painting represents the painter's mental status reflecting the structure and color of the world. A comparison between the result of the text summarization system and the paintings at a particular age indicates the cognitive level of the summarization system. Figure 2.6 shows the comparison between the automatic summarization result (six sentences) of the case study, the painting of a 7-year-old child, and some ancient paintings. This intuitive comparison indicates that the text summarization system is still at the level of collage representation at most, which can be regarded as a simple near decomposable system.

In some cases, reading is to obtain and share knowledge (especially in mathematics) to solve problems or interpret phenomena, while in some cases reading is just to get an impression, especially when reading literary works. To enable readers

[1] The Rc (i) returns a set of the nodes that are the candidates of the root nodes in sentence i. 0
[2] We denote by rij the variable that is one if word i j is selected as a root of an extracting sentence subtree. 0
[3] We counted the number of sentences in the source document that each method used to generate a summary 5 5 Note that the number for the EDU method is not equal to selected textual units because a sentence in the source document may contain multiple EDUs. 0
[4] The sentence tree is a tree that has words as nodes and head modifier relationships between words obtained by the dependency parser as edges.   1
[5] We can build the nested tree by regarding each node of the document tree as a sentence tree.   1
[6] Our method jointly utilizes relations between sentences and relations between words, and extracts a rooted document subtree from a document tree whose nodes are arbitrary subtrees of the sentence tree.   1

Figure 2.6 An intuitive comparison between automatic summarization result and ancient paintings. Up-left: collage of rock carvings at Bronze Age (https://en.wikipedia.org/wiki/ Nordic_Bronze_Age). Up-right: Dunhuang wall painting (http://public.dha.ac.cn, the pattern was popular in the Han dynasty, 206 BC-220 AD). Low-left: a painting of a 7-year-old modern Chinese child (Sirui Zhuge). Low-right: a result of summarization.

to obtain interesting impressions will be a function of future summarization. An interesting impression usually has no a clear goal and interpretation. A collage is a simple way to form a structure and it is also a way to indicate an impression. The key to provide an interest impression is to model the interests of different users and maintain the models through lifetime. The semantic structures underlying readers' reading histories reflect their interests to a certain extent.

To accurately predict individual interest, a system also needs the supporting data from social dimension, reflecting career stage, economic status, social relations, culture, ..., etc.

2.11 Semantic link

The structure of text emerges with the interaction between representation components through various relations. Simon's propositions emphasize on the aggregation relation, which is an *is-part-of* link. More semantic links such as sequential link and cause-effect link connect system behaviors. A semantic link network is a model of a semantic web of data, which can be either small data or big data. The semantic link network model ([139−141], and [142]) needs to consider the views of users. In some applications, especially big data applications, users can have different views on the semantic links between data.

2.11.1   Uncertainty on semantic link

Various semantic links that connect representation components of different scales are the basic semantic structure that helps representation and understanding. Such a semantic structure can be a map that guides summarization. The explicit citation between papers is certain while the semantic links between natural language representation components (e.g., word, sentence and paragraph) are uncertain in general because:

1. The meaning of various representations is uncertain. People often experience misunderstanding when emailing and chatting online.
2. The way of representation (e.g., natural language) is flexible. There are multiple ways to represent the same meaning.
3. Writers have differences on the knowledge of content and the knowledge of representation (e.g., natural language representation) and have different styles of representation.
4. Readers have differences on the knowledge of the contents and the knowledge of representation for understanding the representation.
5. Writers and readers may have different cultural backgrounds to represent and understand. Readers can understand the writers in the same culture more easily.

Considering the uncertainty of data, a semantic link between data takes place with some probabilities as follows:

A—(r_1, p_1), (r_2, p_2), ..., (r_n, p_n)—B, where A and B denote representation components, and (r_k, p_k) denotes a relation r_k between two representation components with probability p_k ($k = 1, 2, ..., n$), and $p_1 + p_2 + ... + p_n \leq 1$. A representation component may link to multiple representation components.

A rule on semantic links takes the following form:

A—(r_1, p_1), (r_2, p_2), ..., (r_m, p_m)—B, B—(r_1, q_1), (r_2, q_2), ..., (r_n, q_n)—$C \Rightarrow A$—(r_1, t_1), (r_2, t_2), ..., (r_n, t_n)—C, where p_k, q_k and t_k are probabilities, $p_1 + p_2 + ... + p_n \leq 1$, $q_1 + q_2 + ... + q_n \leq 1$, $t_1 + t_2 + ... + t_n \leq 1$, and $p_k * r_k = t_k$ ("*" denotes a relational operation).

The semantic links in text and the rules on the semantic links provide a semantic map for representing and understanding [142]. *The general semantic links in representation (e.g., text) and the rules on the semantic links provide a context for interpreting summarization.* For example, if the instance link, explanation link, and implication link can be identified, the instances, further explanations and implicated representations could be considered as less important when making a summarization. If a representation can be transformed into a semantic link network, summarization becomes a problem of generalizing the network or finding a sub-graph of the network that matches the user's interest.

2.11.2   Bias on semantic link

Another type of uncertainty of semantic link is due to different opinions from users. It is natural to have different views for people who live in different societies and have different worldviews. This is why the category hierarchy in Wikipedia has loops and contradicted super/sub-category relations. So, it is necessary to add users to semantic links. The following is a way to incorporate users into semantic links:

A—(r_1, p_1)—B / u, or A—(r_1, p_1)—B / $\{u_1, ..., u_n\}$, where "/" means the relation A—(r_1, p_1)—B is agreed by a user u or a group of users $\{u_1, ..., u_n\}$.

So, some contradicted super/sub-category relations like *Natural Science* →
Science and *Science* → *Natural Science* in Wikipedia can be resolved as follows:
Natural Science → *Science/u₁* and *Science* → *Natural Science/u₂*.

Reasoning rules on semantic links only hold for the same group of users. For
example:

$A—r_1—B/U_1, A—r_1—B/U_2 \Rightarrow A—r_1—B/U_1 \cup U_2.$
$A—r_1—B/U_1, B—r_1—C/U_2,$ and r_1 is transitive $\Rightarrow A—r_1—C/U_1 \cap U_2.$

It is particular significant to incorporate users into semantic links for a large-
scale semantic link network with diverse users because the links connect not only
representations but also users. This adds a condition to realizing accurate content
services such as interpretation, searching, recommendation, question answering and
summarization because user information (e.g., interest), user-relevant information
(e.g., social network) and user-oriented strategies (e.g., the strategies for grouping
users) can be used for accurate services.

Texts for summarization are not isolated. There are explicit semantic links (e.g.,
citations, coauthors, ..., etc.) and implicit semantic links between texts (e.g.,
sharing words or phrases). Texts have authors and readers who request, make and
use summarizations. Authors and readers are semantically linked through texts and
the social networks they involve in.

The semantic link network within a text renders the content. The semantic link
network of texts renders the context of the text. The semantic link network of people models a society where individuals read and write texts, express interests and
evolve communities. The three-tier semantic link networks co-evolve to emerge a
complex structure for summarization and interpretations as depicted in Figure 2.7.

2.11.3 Separation of semantic link networks

In general, a semantic link is a relational representation that connects two representations, supports interpretation and reasoning with other links and facilitates predictive operations on representations [141]. There are two major differences between
hyperlink and semantic link: (1) hyperlink is based on address (URL) while semantic link is based on content (this implies that semantic links can be automatically

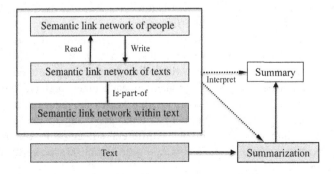

Figure 2.7 The summarization context based on the three-tier semantic link networks.

established according to the linked contents and reasoning on semantic links), and (2) hyperlink is for humans to browse (through language label) while semantic link is not only for humans to read but also for machines to connect and reason.

Various semantic link networks evolve when people experience in the complex space consisting of cyberspace, physical space and social space.

1. *The semantic link networks about representations* are weaved through interactions between various language components. The most basic link reflects the co-occurrence relation like that between neighboring words and that co-occur in readers' eyes. The sequential link reflects the time order, for example, the order of writing and reading sentences. More semantic links are discussed in [140−142].
2. *The semantic link networks about facts are waved through co-occurred representations.* The happening of facts does not rely on human sensory. A fact (e.g., people on the same flight) takes place no matter whether people know it or not. The semantic link network about facts is usually temporal so it is recorded through devices.
3. *The semantic link networks about cognition.* Humans understand facts or representations through experiencing, talking, writing, reading, and reasoning. For example, two persons will emerge a fact about taking the same flight in mind when they meet and talk about their travel experience, which is involved in the same thing at the same time. This type of semantic link networks often emerge when people are reading novels and watching movies. People evolve personal semantic link networks in minds, which leads to the diversity of understanding, thinking and behavior.

Various semantic link networks emerge separately and co-evolve their structures in different spaces while human experience in the complex space consisting of cyberspace, physical space and social space. Semantic communities emerge and evolve with the evolution of the semantic link network [139]. Wikipedia provides an evolving repository of commonsense for mapping and interpreting semantic links empirically.

2.12 Summary

The main motivation of this chapter is to answer the following questions: *What are the principles and rules for emerging the structure of text as a near decomposable system? How do the principles and rules influence summarization?*

The basic assumption of this work is that various representation components have differences in contributing to the structure of a text and the formation of the structure significantly influences the differences.

Human summarization is about knowledge, understanding and language use while automatic summarization concerns the modeling of text. There are two streams of models on texts: one stream (including the vector space model and topic model) assumes that words are independent of each other, and the other stream (including semantic link network) assumes that words are inter-related to render themes (this work distinguishes theme from topic according to the semantic link point of view). Human reading involves different strategies in different cases. Integrating the two streams of models is a way to establish a powerful model for summarization.

Structure and functions are two aspects of a system. To accurately represent the semantics of a flexible representation is difficult. A static structure of texts localizes the representation and understanding of semantics, but it does not represent semantics. An emerging and evolving near decomposable structure is a way to interpret semantics with the process of the formation and evolution of structure. The case study shows that the principles and rules of emerging the structure of text help improve text summarization, and incorporating more relations into the emerging process can improve summarization but not to a great extent. This shows that the emerging structure can help representation and understanding but it is still limited in ability to accurately represent semantics. Building the semantic link network of representation components of different scales is a way to reflect semantics through modeling richer internal structure, but it still cannot accurately represent semantics.

This research raises a new question: *What is the key issue of automatic summarization*? Observing human summarization tells us that human summarization relies on knowledge rather than word-level processing. A simple example is that it is difficult for people who know little about artificial intelligence to summarize a research paper on artificial intelligence. What makes it difficult? It is the level of knowledge on artificial intelligence, especially the basic concepts and some patterns beyond the paper.

The following chapter will discuss the basic structures—patterns—in representation and understanding, and will seek the answer: *What makes a system decomposable*?

Patterns in representation and understanding

3

A pattern is a kind of regularity in a representation space. It involves objective aspects and subjective aspects. The pattern in a set of physical objects reflects objective regularity. The objects leave images in mind when humans observe and understand them. These images emerge patterns during understanding and thinking. The patterns in mind are subjective, reflecting the objective patterns, but vary with the dimensions in mind and change of interest. Patterns at a high abstraction level are formed through long-term interactions with a common worldview within a society and influence the formation and evolution of patterns at the lower abstraction level. The pattern in a set of objects evolves with the change of the objects. The patterns in minds evolve with the change and the change of interest through interactions in cyber-physical society. The evolution of patterns influences the way of thinking, representing and understanding.

3.1 Patterns in text

As an intelligent behavior, human summarization involves two related behaviors: (1) *representing, which includes such behaviours as observing, memorising, writing and reading*; and, (2) *understanding, which includes such behaviors as linking a new representation to the existing representations, reasoning on the semantic link networks of representations, and the interpretation of representations according to semantic links and rules.* Patterns of different scales facilitate representation and understanding of that scale. At the sentence scale, patterns are used to compose words to construct sentences, for example, "subject verb," "subject verb direct object," "subject verb indirect object direct object," and "adjunct subject verb indirect object direct object adjunct." Some patterns are at larger scales.

Representing and understanding accompany the process of emerging the patterns in mind and matching between the objective patterns and the subjective patterns, and evolving the patterns in mind. To gain the abilities of representation and understanding in language, students are often requested by teachers to write summaries by reading articles, then teachers often evaluate their summaries according to some basic dimensions reflecting people's interest. For example, a summary of an event should be on three dimensions: (1) the time when the event happens, (2) the location where the event happens, and (3) the people who participated in the event. These dimensions also help automatically detect an event in text by identifying the words about time, location and people.

People often regulate some patterns of representation to facilitate understanding when communities are formed and evolved under some common assumptions

Multi-Dimensional Summarization in Cyber-Physical Society. DOI: http://dx.doi.org/10.1016/B978-0-12-803455-2.00003-2

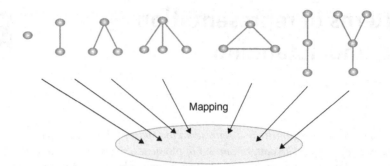

Figure 3.1 Basic patterns and complex patterns: mapping from structure into category space.

for particular purposes, for example in science, engineering, and arts. Scientists have formed patterns for papers, which facilitate representation of thinking and understanding.

There are some basic patterns that are independent of application domains. They are connected as integral basic components and can be composed to form complex patterns. The following are two basic patterns that widely exist:

1. *Object*, which represents an integral physical object, event or abstract concept.
2. *Tuple*, two objects are linked through a binary relation.

Objects and relations are indicated by name space (nouns or noun phrases in texts) while the interpretation of objects and relations needs a mapping from the name space into a category space, which defines objects.

Some more patterns can be generated by composing the basic patterns as depicted in Figure 3.1. For example, *triple* is a pattern composed by linking one object to one of the objects of a tuple, and *tree* is a pattern composed by linking more objects to one of the objects of a triple. The content of the above paragraph contains a triple structure (basic pattern, object, tuple) and the content of a paper contains a tree structure (title, sections, paragraphs). Some patterns have no core while some have cores (e.g., the nodes in red color). Some patterns in social networks like polygons can be also composed by basic patterns, but they do not often appear in texts. Why? One interpretation from cognitive efficiency is that the representation and understanding of them take longer time than simple structures.

Pattern plays the key role in representing and understanding. From the constructionism point of view, patterns can be used to construct new patterns. A near decomposable structure is constructed bottom-up by using basic patterns.

Interpretable Principle of Pattern Composition: *Given a mapping from the pattern space into the category space and for any pattern there is a corresponding category that interprets the pattern, the composition of two patterns is interpretable if the result of composition has a corresponding category in the category space.*

This principle requests that any pattern should be able to be epitomized as a category. If a pattern can be mapped into two or more corresponding categories, these categories should be able to generalized as one category. This ensures the interpretability of a new pattern.

Representativeness: *Representativeness is about the set of objects that renders a pattern.*

1. *For two patterns rendered by the same set of objects, the composition of two patterns has a global representativeness if the result of composition is rendered by all objects of the set (appearance of one exceptional object leads to the change of pattern).*
2. *For two patterns rendered by two sets of objects, the composition of two patterns has a global representativeness if the result of composition is rendered commonly by all objects of the two sets (one exceptional object that participates in rendering the pattern leads to the change of the pattern). The composition of two patterns has partial representativeness if the result of composition can be rendered by one of the two sets.*

This principle interprets why people can compose and understand complex representations. For text composition, some words are used to connect sentence patterns to construct complex sentences, for example: "because," "since," and "so that" represent cause/effect relation; "although," "even though," "though," "whereas," and "while" represent comparison/contrast relation; "where," "wherever," "how," and "however" represent place/manner relation; "if," "whether," and "unless" represent possibility/conditions relation; "that," "which," "who," and "whom" represent the relation of further explanation; and "after," "as," "before," "since," "when," "whenever," "while," and "until" represent time relation.

The pattern shared by a set of decomposable systems represents some natural characteristics of the systems. From the analysis point of view, the above principle indicates the following proposition, where a simpler pattern has fewer nodes and links.

Proposition: *A pattern is a basic pattern or it can be decomposed into simpler patterns with fewer nodes and links.*

Individuals have differences in representing and using languages. It is more desirable to find some patterns within the texts written by the same mature author, for example, find the patterns in all papers of a well-known scientist, or find some patterns within a mature area of research.

One pattern in scientific publication is that scientists summarize their ideas as abstracts placed before the main texts in papers so that readers can quickly know the main idea before reading the main text. A little different from research papers, survey papers summarize previous works on a particular research area, forming the hubs of the knowledge flowing through a network of publications and researchers [135]. Researchers gain the ability through reading and writing to represent and summarize their own research following the patterns.

The abilities of summarization, representation and understanding are enhanced through language learning, using and understanding. Scientists are specialized in summarizing research achievements while journalists are specialized in summarizing events as news in some attractive forms. A text can be understood from different patterns because of the nature of language use and understanding.

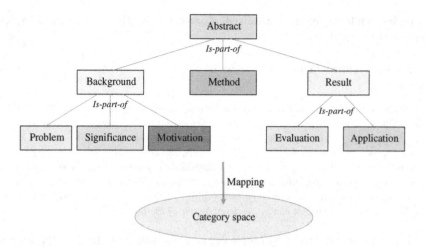

Figure 3.2 The pattern of the abstract of scientific papers and its image in the category space.

Humans established the links between language representations and image representations through experience, and so have the ability to make summarizations using image and language. For example, people can write summaries after attending conferences, watching movies, visiting museums and traveling in the physical space. Summarization provides people (from novices to experts) with more general representation or the interested representation.

The abstract of a scientific paper contains a pattern, which normally consists of the background (concerning problem, significance, or motivation), method, and result (concerning evaluation or applications) so that researchers can easily represent and understand what papers convey. Figure 3.2 depicts the tree pattern of abstract and the mapping from the structure into a category space to obtain interpretation. It is a natural idea to realize automatic text summarization by designing the appropriate patterns for specific applications and by designing the corresponding methods for specializing the patterns of the original texts or the pattern after operations (e.g., generalization) on the existing patterns.

3.2 Pattern mappings

Some patterns are explicit like various standards made by communities, while some are implicit like the knowledge flow in science, which needs discovery within scientific documents.

The following are ways of mapping patterns:

1. *Empirical observation, rational thinking and standardization.* Some standard patterns are formed when a community becomes mature. Rational thinking helps make generalizations on patterns. Standardization like scientific publications enables the patterns to be widely used.
2. *Reasoning.* Some implicit relations can be derived from existing relations through relational reasoning. The derived relations may lead to the discovery of patterns.

3. *Interaction between humans and machines.* Humans mark the pattern in a set of selected texts and train programs to identify the patterns within new texts.

4. *Modeling based on data.* Some statistical models are useful and can be verified within a certain range of data, but in many cases it is hard to prove the models.

For language representation, rhetorical structures have been used to connect language representations, for example, "*some* people use the purchasers' index as a leading indicator, *some* use it as a coincident indicator." To study the rhetorical structure in text is a way to understand the organization of language units within text [76].

The pattern within text is the natural specification for making summarization because patterns reflect the commonsense of people (e.g., researchers of an area) in representation and understanding. Scientific papers have a standard pattern: "Title—abstract—introduction—sections—conclusion—references", which provides a general guidance for summarization.

Patterns in text systems can be an intelligent preference semantics system, which includes analytic knowledge and inductive knowledge of the course of events in the real world, and the methods for transforming necessary knowledge into a canonical template and endeavoring to create semantic chains of nonreductive inferences from the unknowns to the possible referents [127].

3.3   Pattern-based summarization

One way to make a summarization is to find patterns through the analysis of language using behaviors and understanding behaviors, and then use the patterns to generate summaries. Without experience, it is hard for an automatic mechanism to generate such a pattern. Figure 3.3 depicts a summarization method that extracts sentences according to the characteristics of different parts of the pattern and the length of summary required by readers.

A more general pattern of scientific paper is "problem—method—solution". Summarization for this pattern needs the identification and extraction of problem,

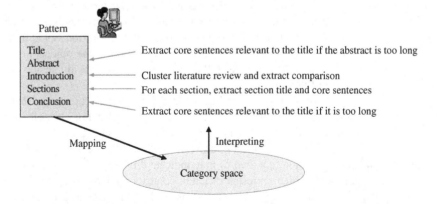

Figure 3.3 Summarizing scientific papers by using the patterns within paper.

method and solution through necessary generalization and specialization. In a mature area, the major problems such as knowledge representation and reasoning in knowledge-based systems have been defined. Researchers usually use phrases to identify their research themes or problems. So, it is a way to make a summarization in the mature areas by making use of the phrases and the phrases appearing in the statements of themes or problems to identify the problems of research, and then making a summarization according to the indicators of the themes or problems.

Patterns have been widely used not only in scientific publication, but also in many other mature fields such as in literature and art, which have implicit patterns compared to those in scientific publications. Different areas usually focus on different features, which may change at different development stages. For example, the Western oil paintings place more emphasis on light and color although there are different ways of expression at different development stages, while Chinese paintings place more emphasis on symbolism.

Recognizing patterns in cyberspace, physical space and social space is a part of human intelligence. Some patterns are explicit, some are implicit, and some are between explicit and implicit. Discovering the implicit patterns is one of the tasks of sciences. Patterns help representation and understanding because they provide guidance for composing various representation units and facilitating the match between representations, e.g., the match between the external representation and the internal representation.

3.4   Incorporating locations into pattern

Patterns can be rendered with different scales, for example, the pattern of sentence and the pattern of a style of text. For a set of texts on the same theme, patterns may be rendered by all texts or by different subsets. The introduction to a research area will be distributed onto the introduction section of all papers within this area. So, a way to summarize a research area is to summarize the introduction section of all papers within the area. Different methods for solving problems within this area may be distributed onto the main bodies of different subsets of the papers. A way to summarize a method is to select the subset of the papers on the method and summarize the subsets.

Geographical location has been widely used in information services because all surface objects are on geographical locations. A geographical location holds a set of physical objects and is connected to the information relevant to the objects in the cyberspace through various sensors like GPS. Location provides a dimension for specifying the context of the objects.

Location is also a dimension for specifying and studying people, contents and texts. People have interests at the locations where they played some roles. For example, one person has different interests when he/she is in restaurant, theater, sport center, and lecture room. Location was widely used to provide location-aware services in mobile computing. One representation (e.g., word) may indicate different meanings at different locations within text, which represent different contexts. The vector space model reflects a pattern of term frequency on a set of texts. A theme may be distributed onto the similar locations of different texts. One text can render one theme or more themes. One person can be the author or the reader of one text or more texts.

Location in the physical space specifies physical objects, location in textual representation indicates the role of a language representation unit like word, and location in mind indicates the location defined by the dimensions of memory if the mind is a multidimensional space. Some implicit links between the physical location and the location in language representation can be discovered through the links between the physical location and the location in mental space (e.g., common interests emerge when people are in particular physical locations such as library and restaurant) and the links between the locations of representation units in representation and the locations in mental space.

The following basic proposition is about location that holds various objects. For example, the students of the same school are likely to be largely the same age or to live in the same region. Objects in the same house usually have the same owner, at least the objects share the same location.

Proposition: *Objects at the same location in the same space share the same or related attributes.*

The following are some implications:

1. Objects often held by the same location have high probability to render the same theme. For example, tables and chairs of the same house, flowers in the same vase, and sentences within the same paragraph.
2. One object can be easily accessed from another object at the same location. As the objects are at the same location, it is easy to access one from the other without consuming more energy. For example, one sentence can be easily read after reading another sentence within the same paragraph, that is why people organize relevant sentences to render the same theme within the same paragraph. This is a kind of locality, which will be discussed in the following chapters.
3. If one person often interacts with one object, he/she has high probability to interact with another object held by the same location. For example, a person has a high probability to talk to the neighbor of a friend, and reading one sentence, a person is likely to read another sentence within the same paragraph.
4. People interacting with the objects at the same location have high probability to interact with each other. For example, readers of the same book have higher probability to interact with each other than readers of different books.

3.5 From psychological dimension

One psychological view of text understanding and recall is that readers will establish representations at three levels:

1. A word-level representation (surface code).
2. A semantics-level representation, which may consist of a microstructure and a macrostructure.
3. A situation-level representation, an integral and coherent representation based on background knowledge [56]. Understanding is a spiral process between the microstructure and the macrostructure.

Another view of text reading is current-state selection, which focuses on the discovery and memory of the cause-effect relations while reading. Some researchers regard text understanding as a problem-solving process by discovering a set of relevant cause-effect relations. Some focus on the importance of the bottleneck of short-term memory in understanding process. Some views incorporate the above two views [36].

Pattern in text is between the word level and the semantics level, reflecting the common features of a class of representations. Patterns help quickly identify the semantics when semantics is difficult to represent.

The formation of pattern reflects the development of the cognition of a community of practice. Pattern will be learned and stored in the long-term memory [33] and can be recalled from the language (including the word-scale) representation that are stored in the short-term memory. This provides an interpretation for the proposition of the independency on integrity given in Chapter 2, The emerging structures.

This inspires thinking about the relation between pattern and system behaviors. For example, long-term interests are more on the patterns of a building, while short-term interests are more on the name of a building; long-term interests are more on the pattern of music, while short-term interests are more on rhythm. Many instances indicate the following proposition:

Proposition: *The long-term behaviors rely more on complex patterns while the short-term behaviors rely more on the basic patterns.*

As the basic patterns are independent of each other, the above proposition provides an interpretation for why the short-term behaviors of subsystems are approximately independent of each other, which is discussed in chapter 2.

3.6 Implications

The first motivation of this chapter is to take a step forward from the discussion of Chapter 2, The emerging structures to answer an important question: *What makes a system decomposable?* Simon used the short-term behavior and long-term behavior as well as the frequency of interaction within components and between components to interpret the features of a near decomposable system. This chapter tries to seek the answer from the internal regularity — *pattern*.

The following is a basic proposition on system. The rationale is that the nature has its pattern regulated by the natural laws (one of the basic assumptions of science) and any artificial system is designed according to a certain principle and method, which regulate the structure and function of a class of systems.

Proposition: *Any system has a pattern.*

Based on this assumption, the following proposition can be drawn from the previous discussion. The basic rationale is that the components of a near decomposable system should keep their own regularities no matter how (e.g., interact more frequently within component than between components, run as a part or independently), when (e.g., long-term or short-term), and what (e.g., function) they perform.

Proposition: *A system is near decomposable if and only if it contains a complex pattern that can be decomposed into several different patterns or it contains duplicated patterns, rendered by different components of the system.*

For example, a research paper contains a complex pattern, which can be decomposed into different patterns rendered by its components: title, abstract, introduction, main text, conclusion and references. A picture can be meaningfully decomposed if and only if it consists of several different patterns or duplicated patterns in different parts.

The second motivation of this chapter is to unveil the intrinsic link between pattern and summarization. Actually, the recognition of the pattern on the input representation is a process of summarization. However, summarization needs to meet personalized requirements. It will facilitate human understanding if the summary contains the same pattern as the original text or contains the pattern that readers are familiar with. If summarization is for application systems to use, the summary should consist of the patterns that are recognizable by the application systems.

This indicates that a summarization system should not be a closed system. A summarization system runs in an environment consisting of the following parts:

1. Humans, including readers and writers.
2. Various application systems, which interact with humans or with each other.
3. The summarization system, which interacts with humans, with other summarization systems (this may need system integration), or with the application systems.
4. Various representations (e.g., texts), which are generated by various systems or by humans, for humans or systems to operate.

Pattern also provides a way to interpret a summary. There are three ways to interpret a summary: (1) use natural language; (2) use the existing patterns; and (3) use existing knowledge, which involves reasoning.

The basis of summarization is that the input representations are interpretable in the summarization environment although there can be different ways to interpret. The representations that are not interpretable should be excluded from the environment. The following definition lays the basis for a meaningful summarization.

Definition: *A representation is interpretable if it can be mapped into a category space shared by the subjects who make interpretation and all its components are interpretable, or it can be mapped into the a pattern that is interpretable.*

The following condition is based on the definition of interpretability and it determines the significance of summarization.

Condition of Summarization: *The representation (e.g., text) to be summarized is interpretable.*

The following proposition is based on this assumption.

Proposition: *A summary is interpretable if (1) it represents the same pattern as the input representation or a component of the pattern of the input representation, and (2) all its components are interpretable.*

However, this does not mean the summarization is interpretable if both input and output are interpretable. The following is a way to define an interpretable summarization.

Definition: *A summarization is interpretable if (1) all outputs represent the same pattern as the inputs; or, (2) it only transforms the pattern of every input into the output that contains the pattern that is interpretable in the environment and the rules for transformation is interpretable (i.e., the rules are existing knowledge or can be derived from the existing knowledge).*

This definition provides a basis for discussing the interpretability of automatic summarization systems from rationalism.

A set of representations can render patterns from different dimensions. The following section will discuss a conceptual model of a multi-dimensional think lens, which can zoom-in and zoom-out on a set of representations and carry out reasoning through multiple dimensions.

The think lens

4

The nature of many research problems is about scale and dimension of observation and thinking. Whether the patterns and rules on one scale still hold on the other scale? Whether the pattern and rules on one dimension or some dimensions still hold on the other dimension or some other dimensions? Summarization is also about the scale and the dimension of motivation, observation, representation and thinking. Human eyes can focus on not only a part of a representation but also the whole from a certain distance like the lens of camera. The think lens is a mechanism that can zoom in and out while observing, searching, mapping, analysing, planning, predicting, calculating, imagine and representing patterns through semantic computing and reasoning on various representations according to some principles and rules. This paper presents a conceptual model of the think lens for realizing general summarization in cyber-physical society.

4.1 The conceptual model

Humans have the ability to change the scale and the dimension of representation during observing, reading, writing, talking, thinking, and representing. The think lens models this ability based on the semantic lens, which was initially proposed to transform the traditional closed computing models into an open interactive semantic computing model [139].

The basic specification of the semantic lens is as follows:

1. *Representation space.* All representations (e.g., text) to be observed through the semantic lens are organized in the representation space with a certain number of dimensions. A representation can be located by its projections at the dimensions.
2. *Input and output.* The input consists of a representation to be observed and an interest representation. The output is a representation that matches the interest representation.
3. *Focus.* It can focus on a part of the representation that matches the interest input.
4. *Zoom.* It can zoom-in and zoom-out to focus on the representation of different scales through different dimensions and different semantic links according to the operations on the scale and dimension. The semantic images (modeled by the semantic link network of concepts) of different scales and dimensions can emerge with zooming along dimensions.
5. *Generalization and specialization.* It can emerge a more general semantic image or a more special semantic image on different dimensions when focusing on a representation.
6. *Coordination.* It can coordinate one semantic image to the other semantic images by selecting appropriate semantic links when emerging semantic images.

Different from the lens of camera, the semantic lens can emerge semantic images while zoom-in and zoom-out to compute the representation of different

Multi-Dimensional Summarization in Cyber-Physical Society. DOI: http://dx.doi.org/10.1016/B978-0-12-803455-2.00004-4

scales and dimensions. From a node of the semantic image, the semantic lens can zoom-out to emerge the linked nodes, and zoom out further to emerge semantic communities (nodes are tightly linked within community and loosely linked between communities [139], i.e., a semantic components of a near decomposable system) of different scales that include the node. Zoom-in a bit emerges its structure. Zoom-in a bit more emerges communities or the connected branches. Zoom-in a bit more, the explicit semantic links and the implicit semantic links that can be derived from the rules emerge. The semantic lens can show the reasoning process step-by-step. Zoom-in further, the interpretations of relevant relations emerge. Zoom-in to the nearest, a node and its attributes emerge. The semantic link network can show different semantic views with only the interested semantic links. Due to the dynamicity and the self-organization nature of the semantic link network, semantic images evolve with time.

In addition to zooming on the self-organized communities on semantic link network, the semantic lens can also zoom on the multi-dimensional representation space as shown in Figure 4.1. The multi-dimensional space enables a semantic lens to focus on a point, on a subspace that contains a part of original dimensions, or on a view that contains a part of original dimensions and a part of coordinates.

In addition to zoom from a node, the semantic lens can also focus on a semantic image within a range by giving a pair of classes or a pair of super-classes on the same generalization chain. For example, [*apple, fruit*] and [*apple, computer*] indicate a sharper semantic image than just a word *apple*. Zoom-in to show more specific semantics by increasing dimensions or going down to the lower level of the

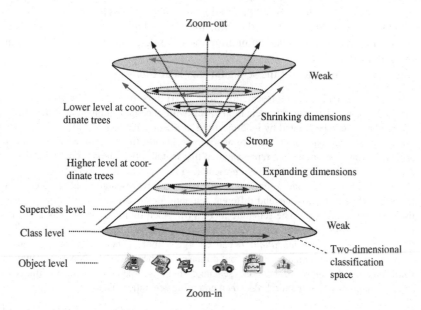

Figure 4.1 The conceptual model of the semantic lens, which zooms on a multi-dimensional category space [138].

category hierarchy at every dimension, zoom-out to show more general semantics by decreasing dimensions or moving to the higher level of the coordinate trees at every dimension (category hierarchy).

Communities of different granularities within a semantic link network can also form category hierarchy. Mapping the nodes or communities in the semantic link network into the points or subspaces of the multi-dimensional category space can integrate the semantic link network and the category space. Therefore, the lens can zoom onto the semantic link network from the category space or zoom onto the category space from the semantic link network.

When focusing on a semantic image, the relevant semantic images emerged in the past can be augmented to reemerge, just like relevant old events emerge when we hear an old song or watch an old movie. Patterns may emerge in the long-term memory. The re-focusing rate can contribute to the weight of a semantic image and then influence other semantic images through semantic links. One distinguished feature of the semantic link network is self-organization: there is no central control on its formation and evolution.

The think lens is a model that simulates human's multidimensional thinking by building reasoning mechanism and multiple views of recognizing the world (including cognition, psychology, complex systems, and language) on the semantic lens. Zooming on different dimensions through different semantic links simulates thinking behaviors through multiple dimensions, including searching, computing, mapping, reasoning, planning, transforming, determining the logic consequences of assumptions, and organizing a decision or an insight.

Summarization can be extended through a think lens based on the semantic link network and multi-dimensional category space as depicted in Figure 4.2. The following are some of its basic semantic link networks:

1. The semantic link network of models enables a semantic lens to interact and manage various representations through different semantic models like the relational data model and the resource space model [139]. Viewing a complex representation as a system, the semantic link network of models actually simulates the system of systems.
2. The semantic link network of languages establishes the mapping between languages to support the translation between languages and the interpretation in different languages.
3. The semantic link network of texts enables individuals to read and write in natural languages through semantic lens so that a piece of text can be viewed from different facets, abstraction levels, scales and versions. Techniques of natural language processing help preprocess texts.
4. The semantic link network of events enables individuals to know one event from the other through semantic links. An event consists of the involved physical objects and human individuals as well as scene, place and time.
5. The semantic link network of physical objects enables the lens to sense one object together with relevant objects and to navigate among objects through semantic links.
6. The semantic link network of human individuals reflects social relations among individuals. The semantic nodes reflect human characteristics.
7. The semantic link network of scenes enables the semantic lens to coordinate scenes so that relevant scenes can emerge when observing one scene. Mappings between scenes, individuals, objects and sounds help coordinate semantic link networks.

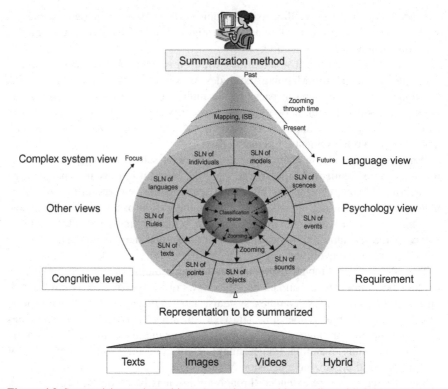

Figure 4.2 Summarizing various objects (texts, images, video, audio and hybrid) through a multi-dimensional think lens on the representations of various objects, cognitive levels and requirements.

8. The semantic link network of sounds reflects such relations as similarity, co-occurrence, cause-effect and coherence between sounds. It enables the semantic lens to sense and make use of sounds based on the mappings between sounds, events, scenes and objects. Nodes in the semantic link networks will be mapped into the points of the category space.

9. The semantic link network of points is a large granularity semantic link network where any point can include objects and information from other channels such as sounds, symbols, events and scenes.

10. The semantic link of rules reflects the relations among rules like the reasoning relation between rules. Reasoning can carry out across different types of semantic link networks.

Through the think lens, a summarization method is able to process the representation of various objects (texts, images, video, audio and hybrid) and the requirements and cognitive levels of users from different dimensions. Through zoom-in and zoom-out operation, the summarization method can generate different summaries from the same input representation.

In cyberspace, existing metadata, information retrieval techniques, statistical techniques, classification techniques, reasoning techniques (relational, inductive and analogical reasoning), text analysis and social network analysis can indicate semantic links but are not sufficient to render rich semantic images, which evolve with constant interaction. Integrating these techniques, studying interaction behaviors, tracing interactions and recording the content of interaction and the co-occurrence scenes, sounds, objects, individuals and events can enrich imaginations when forming semantic images.

Various semantic link networks are coordinated on a basic semantic common sense: the Interactive Semantic Base [139]. The relations between the observer's interest and the following elements are established during the interactions through various semantic links:

1. The formation order of semantic links.
2. Semantic communities.
3. Reasoning on semantic link network.
4. Co-occurrence relation among nodes, semantic links and experiences.
5. Mapping and analogy between semantic link networks [141].
6. Time of nodes' presence.
7. Workflows among semantic nodes.
8. Direct and indirect relation between individuals and between objects.

Showing one type of semantic link network, the think lens emerges relevant types of semantic link networks according to the coordination rules and relations (may be implicit). Semantic nodes and semantic links have corresponding points in the category space on the semantic link. The lens can show semantic images from different dimensions with multiple abstraction levels. The time dimension records the time of interaction, the time of event occurrence, and the time of adding a semantic link to the semantic link network. The time dimension enables the lens to operate semantic images through time.

The current e-presence techniques can capture the videos, photos, audios, texts and their synchronization relations of human presence and replay them according to the synchronization relations. The key issue is how to automatically link diverse types of resources and coordinate semantic link networks according to diverse individuals' interests that may change from time to time. It is difficult if we only know isolated objects. Interactive semantics provides explanation, indication, social relation, generalization, specialization, and interaction mechanism for solving this issue.

Zooming may be navigated between different types of semantic link networks or between points in a category space by changing the focus according to interest. For example, the navigation route can start from the semantic link network of scenes to its communities, to the category space (may change abstraction levels), and then to the semantic link network of sounds. The navigation route can also start from a point in the category space to a semantic link network, and then go back to the category space (may be another point).

When individuals are only interested in the network structure, the central nodes and their communities have the priority of emerge. Different from the centrality principle in the general network, linking a new node or adding a new semantic link to a semantic link network is likely to generate new semantic links due to relational reasoning on semantic links. A new node will be immediately known from relevant nodes within a community through relational reasoning. The centrality emerges not only with the explicit semantic link but also with the potential semantic links generated through reasoning.

4.2   The semantic images of words

Zooming onto word space emerges a semantic link network of words. Humans create words to indicate concepts; one word can be used to indicate multiple concepts, and multiple words can be used to indicate one concept. The use of words creates the links between words. A basic semantic link is *co-occurrence*, which reflects the relation that one word occurs "after" or "before" the other word. A set of words can be semantically linked (e.g., cause-effect link) to another set of words indicating the relation between complex concepts. The category space can be regarded as the semantic link network of categories and a category consists of several concepts. The people space can be regarded as a semantic link network of people, who create words, use words to indicate concepts, and interact with each other to evolve concepts and the usages of words.

Figure 4.3 shows the relations among word space, text space, category space and people space. The category space and word space are not big and relatively stable although new concepts and new words are created from time to time. The people space contains big and dynamic social networks, where nodes are updated from generation to generation. The text space is big and it expands unlimitedly. A text can be regarded as a network of words, which indicates a semantic link

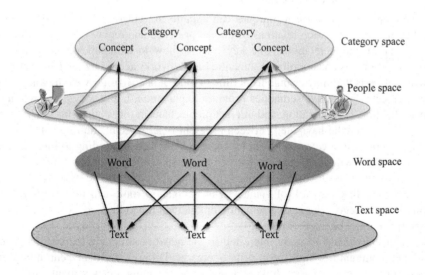

Figure 4.3 The relations among words, texts, concepts and people.

network of concepts. The semantic link network of words and the semantic link of concepts are different in nodes and links because some links between words are about language, e.g., the location of words does not exist in the concept network. For the space of texts, there are two basic measures:

1. *The frequency of word*, which has been widely used in information retrieval. The major advantage of the methods based on word frequency is that the model is simple and the computing process is interpretable. There are three major problems: the big number of words in texts increases the complexity of computation, the frequency of words does not reflect the semantics of words within texts, and one word appearing in different contexts is regarded as the same. Therefore these methods are limited in ability to support semantics-level applications.
2. *The frequency of the link used by people* (e.g., the frequency of one word is used after another), denoted as $W—a→W'$ | (f, u), where W and W' indicate one word or a set of words respectively, a indicates a relation, f indicates the frequency of W' occurred after W, and u indicates user.

For a community of people, the commonly used words are stable, and the link from one word (or word set) to the other word (or word set) is also stable. So the frequency of link is a new way to study the formation of text, especially in personalized word (or phrase) recommendation in a writing environment. The link between words can be extended to the link between phrases or between sentences.

An advanced think lens can have multiple types of outputs, including a piece of language representation that matches the interest representation, a semantic link network of language units (words, phrases, sentences, etc.), and a semantic link network of concepts. The think lens links language representation units to concepts.

Figure 4.4 depicts the mapping from the word space into multiple spaces. Zooming onto one word emerges images in language space, definition space, category space, knowledge space, and experience space. Each space can contain subspaces, for example, the knowledge space contains the theory subspace, the method subspace, and the technology subspace. The language space is a semantic link network of language representation units. Mapping "Artificial" into the language space obtains its language features including the part-of-speech and the words often used together such as "intelligence," "flower," "life," "machine," and "human." The experience space provides real-world experience for words. For example, people who have visited Cairo and Giza will generate richer images in their minds of the word "pyramid" than before they knew the details such as the weight and the size of the stones, the distance between pyramids, the temperature, the city environment, and the local culture. The social space provides the social situations including the relationship between people and economic status of the society for the word.

A semantic image of the word as a point in one space can link to the semantic images as points in the other spaces to render complex images. For example, people can link the experience space to the language space and the physical space to render a more precise semantic image on the pyramids. The cyber representation of these spaces is the key to enable computing systems to understanding human representations.

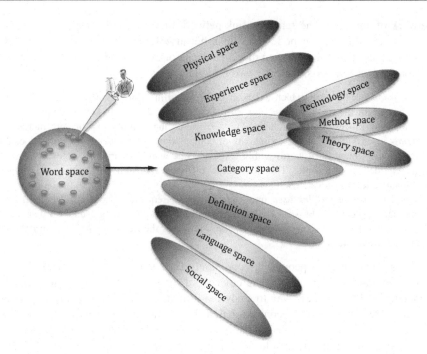

Figure 4.4 Zooming onto a word emerges semantic images in multiple spaces.

Humans can map the external representation into the internal mental representation, which evolves through experience and internal operations such as memory, recall, association, thinking, verification, and the formation of categories. Words are the basic units of the traditional natural language processing techniques. Mapping words into multiple spaces to build cyber-concepts is the basis of realizing an advanced intelligent system.

The implementation of the conceptual model of the think lens needs the innovation of some basic computing techniques. The semantic link network of concepts and the multi-dimensional category space are candidate models but they need to develop towards an automatic construction and self-adaptive system:

1. Automatic construction of semantic link network of concepts. The following issues need to be considered:
   a. The representation of concept. One approach is to regard concept as a service, a more active modeling of concept, with an interface consisting of inputs and outputs and operations. This book uses category to represent a category of concepts.
   b. Discovering implicit semantic rules and developing the methods for reasoning and interpretation.
   c. Developing the mechanism of integrating relational reasoning, deductive reasoning, analogical reasoning, and inductive reasoning.
   d. The analysis of the semantic link networks.
   e. The interpretation of semantic link network of concepts. Categories at one abstraction level can be used to interpret the categories at another abstraction level. One form of representation can be used to interpret the other form of representation.

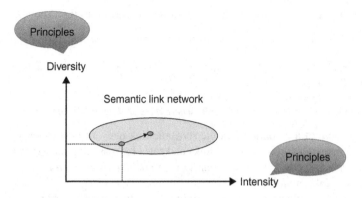

Figure 4.5 Measuring semantic link network in a multi-dimensional space.

2. *Adaptive multi-dimensional category space.* Given a set of texts, different partitioning methods form different dimensions, each of which can be a category hierarchy. These dimensions provide multiple perspectives for understanding and managing this set of texts. The expansion of texts requests the evolution of the space, reflecting the evolution of the concepts shared by the authors. With the category hierarchy, a concept can inherit the existing concepts predefined in the category hierarchy, and then can be enriched through reading, writing and reasoning.

4.3 The principle of emerging semantic images

The think lens emerges semantic images according to some principles and measures.

The page rank widely used in the World Wide Web focuses on the intensity of connection. It reflects a philosophy of "the more, the better" and "the rich gets richer," where "more" and "rich" represent a measure on one dimension: the number of properties occupied by an individual. However, there are some different philosophies, for example, the philosophy of "less is more."

Diversity plays an important role in driving the sustainable development of society and ecosystems. Diversity can be measured on many dimensions. Diversity in semantics is another dimension of driving the evolution of a semantic link network.

A measure of richness can be defined on two dimensions: *intensity* and *diversity*, as shown in Figure 4.5. Each dimension holds some principles. The richness of a point in the space is a function of diversity and intensity.

From the proposition of cooperative linking introduced in Section 4.2, the richness of node and link within a semantic link network can be defined as follows.

The richness of a semantic node is in positive proportion to the following components:

1. *The number and the diversity of the semantic links the node has.*
2. *The richness of the node's neighbors.*
3. *The richness of the community the node locates.*

The richness of a semantic link is in positive proportion to the following factors:

1. *The number and the richness of the semantic links that the semantic link can interact (reasoning) with.*
2. *The global impact of the semantic link (e.g., the times the semantic link appeared) within the whole network.*
3. *The richness of the two connected nodes.*
4. *The richness of the semantic community where the semantic link locates in.*

The richness of a community in the semantic link network is rendered by the richness of its semantic nodes, semantic links and rules for reasoning on semantic links. *The richness of a semantic community is in positive proportion to the richness of its semantic links, nodes, and rules.*

The richness reflects a complex driving force to evolve the semantic link network. A richer semantic link contributes more to the richness of the linked nodes, and a richer node contributes more to the richness of its linked semantic links. To become rich, a new node should *link to enrich semantic links*, that is, the new semantic link should be relevant to the potential neighbor semantic links. This is different from the preference attachment effect of the hyperlink network of the World Wide Web: *a new node tends to link to a high-rank node.*

A semantic link network may have multiple semantic paths between semantic nodes. Which path takes the priority to emerge? From the dimension of cognitive efficiency: *The less information a semantic path contains, the easier people understand and remember.* This indicates the following simplest emerging principle:

Simplest Emerging Principle: *The shortest path with the least types of semantic links takes the priority to emerge as the semantics of the relation between two nodes.*

This can be explained by Shannon and Weiner's theory of information entropy: the lower entropy a path has, the less semantic link type it contains. Therefore it can be more easily understood. The simplest emerging principle focuses on a particular semantic path while the massive emerging principle emphasizes the status of a semantic node or a semantic link within the whole network.

A principle of emerging lies in the long-term behaviors. For the near decomposable systems, the long-term behaviors of components are interrelated and cooperatively contribute to the general system function. A component similar to another component will be assimilated or eliminated from the system in the long-term for the efficiency of the whole system.

Distinguished Principle: *The semantic image of community/individual/object/relation takes the priority to emerge if it is distinguished from others for long-term behaviors.*

The following are some instances of the principle. The original papers will take the priority to emerge and similar papers will be eliminated during the evolution of the citation network. A researcher whose research achievement is distinguished from others takes the priority to emerge among researchers. On the other hand, if a researcher has many papers on one topic, other researchers can usually cite one or two of the author's papers. So, to emerge within the citation network, a researcher should distinguish his/her research from others and his/her own papers should be distinguished from each other (e.g., publishing in different areas is a way to be distinguished).

To be distinguished, an individual or a community needs to maintain the distinguished characteristics. A humanized Cyber-Physical Society should enable any individual to autonomously select appropriate friends, and enable any community to maintain an appropriate structure. To do this, individual and community should be able to predict situations and to actively select new semantic links. This is different from the World Wide Web, where Web pages cannot prevent themselves from being linked. The distinguished principle provides a strategy for the poor individuals to take the priority of emerging.

Within a semantic link network, one node links to another node to render communities, evolving the semantic link network into a decomposable system. The priority of emerging inevitably propagates through semantic links for long-term behaviors. The relevance principle is a kind of relevance priority that reflects the phenomenon: the emerging semantic image draws the emerging of another semantic image through semantic links.

Relevance Principle: *A semantic image takes the priority of emerging if it links to an emerging semantic image with a semantic link or an implicit semantic link through possible reasoning. A richer semantic link renders the higher priority.*

The think lens is a general computing mechanism for observing and interacting various representations in the cyberspace, physical space, and social space through multiple dimensions, which can help realize general summarization.

The following chapter will take a further step toward a multi-dimensional methodology.

Multi-dimensional methodology   5

The ability to understand and think through dimensions is an important part of human intelligence. Automatically discovering dimensions on resources provides multi-dimensional perspectives for efficiently and effectively operating resources. Different methodologies guide people to understand and think through different dimensions. Multi-dimensional methodology is a space of various methodologies that can manage, coordinate, map, and compose methodologies as well as guide applications and predict development.

5.1 Dimension

Humans have created various spaces while living in the physical space. Some spaces are physical such as cities, buildings and homes, which contain various forms of objects and the relations between objects. The dimensions of the space like time and location provide the measures for recognizing and managing various objects. Some spaces are mathematic spaces like Euclidean space and Hilbert space. Some spaces are cyberspace like the World Wide Web and the Internet of Things. Some spaces are hybrid like Cyber-Physical Society. In the meanwhile, humans build various dimensions in minds to help observe and think through various dimensions.

Humans have used dimensions to manage resources in various spaces. Some dimensions like latitude and longitude are closed, some dimensions like research areas are open. A hierarchical dimension can scale-up and scale-down according to application requirements. Discovering the dimensions of complex systems such as economic systems and cities needs exploration through analyzing big numbers of features, generalizing dimensions and validating dimensions in practice.

Artists have represented the impressions of various spaces on two-dimensional surfaces by using lines, curves and colors, therefore transforming explicit measures of dimension into implicit measures. Figure 5.1 shows a space of paintings with dimensions: *type* (*oil, water-color, etc.*), *time*, and *author*. The two paintings reflect the impression of perspectives of a café terrace at night in Vincent van Gogh's mind, which is different from the photos taken by camera, reflecting physical features. However, the three dimensions are limited in ability to represent emotions, i.e., the two paintings represent different emotions. To measure emotion, one more dimension, *emotion*, needs to be added to the space through coordinating the other two dimensions: any painting has a projection at every dimension.

For the space of university job ads, *subject*, *university*, *location*, and *position* (*professor, associate professor, assistant professor*) are its dimensions, by which

Multi-Dimensional Summarization in Cyber-Physical Society. DOI: http://dx.doi.org/10.1016/B978-0-12-803455-2.00005-6

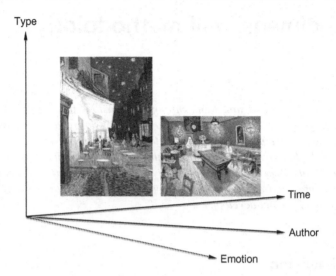

Figure 5.1 "Cafe at Night" (left) and "The Nigh Café" (right), 1888 by Vincent van Gogh.

people can quickly search the interested jobs. For a space of enterprises, *the pattern of organization, product, people* (*employer, employee, customer, supplier*), *process* (*production process, supply chain, quality process*), and *technology* are candidate dimensions.

The dimensions specify the structure of a space, representing the understanding of the observed objects. Different dimensions represent different views of understanding the observed objects. A subspace is specified by fewer number of dimensions. A dimension can be regarded as a subspace with just one dimension.

The dimensions on a set of objects concern the subjective view and the objective view.

1. *From the subjective view*, the dimensions of viewing the objects in the world represent the way to recognize the world. For example, the customers of different ages, professions and economic statuses may provide comments on hotels from different views such as *service, facility, location*, and *price*. Different views represent different concerns on the overall data of hotels. For a search engine, its users express different search requirements. These search requirements can be categorized so that different categorizations represent different views on the data indexed in the search engine. Actually, these different views represent the dimensions on the data from diverse usage requirements.

2. *From the objective view*, dimensions represent the clusters of the natural features of a set of objects. For example, the *color, shape* and *weight* of a set of physical objects can be regarded as different dimensions on these objects. The time and location of a set of events taken place can be regarded as two dimensions on these events. The recognition of the natural features is based on the categorization of the data sensed from the physical objects.

The subjective dimensions change with the development of human recognition about the world. Significant change will happen with new members constantly joining the existing groups of observers. The objective view is relatively stable, but in the long run, the objective dimensions will change with the significant change of the subjective dimensions, for example, new measures are invented to identify the new features of objects. People interact with each other in a lifetime and can establish and evolve consensus on dimensions through the development of society, so the following proposition is rational:

Proposition: *The separation of subjective dimensions and objective dimensions on the same set of objects tends to reduce if both the community of the observers and the set of objects are stable for long term.*

However, the subjective dimensions will change when both the community of observers and the set of objects are dynamic. People are usually limited in time and energy to identify the changing big data.

Figure 5.2 depicts the formation of the subjective dimension and the objective dimension. Different ways to form dimensions support different methods for managing the objects. The method based on the subjective dimensions tends to find the consensus of the observers. For example, the categories in Wikipedia reflect the subjective consensus of contributors. The method based on the objective dimensions tends to find the natural attributes of the objects and cluster the attributes using objective measures. For example, the time, author, affiliation and publisher are attributes of papers. For the near decomposable systems, the dimensions on components are usually different from the dimensions on the systems. The is-part-of relation between components and systems establishes the relation between the spaces of different granularities.

The combination of the subjective dimension and the objective dimension is a way to form a more complete set of dimensions for people to understand objects and

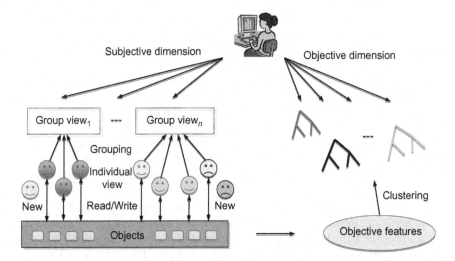

Figure 5.2 The integration of subjective dimension and the objective dimension.

manage objects effectively. Therefore, the research method is different from the method in natural science, which explores the nature following the objective criteria. ACM Computing Classification System can be regarded as the integration of the subjective dimension and the objective dimension because the formation of categories is natural and humans standardize the categories based on consensus. The standards need to be updated when the objects have been significantly changed, e.g., when a new research area emerges with the publication of a certain number of closely related papers.

Human individuals or social organizations can also be abstracted as objects when human behaviors or organization behaviors are observed and studied. The features of human individuals or organizations in the cyberspace, physical space and social space can be clustered as objective dimensions, which help humans to understand themselves when observing the objects. Discovering dimensions enables computing systems to interact with humans through appropriate dimensions. For example, building multi-dimensional interest models for users enables different users to interact with computing systems in a complex space consisting of cyberspace, physical space and psychological space.

5.2 Category

One concept closely related to dimension is category, which has different definitions in philosophy, mathematics, linguistics, and computer science.

Aristotle defined ten categories to classify all things. The primary categories are substance, relation, quantity, and quality. The secondary categories are place, time, situation, condition, action, and passion. The ten categories were reduced to five categories (substance, relation, quantity, motion and quality), and then reduced to two categories: substance and relation. In the twentieth century some philosophers moved from the metaphysics of categorization towards the linguistic problem of defining the words being used. One of the fundamental problems of ontology is to classify existing things into appropriate categories.

Different from philosophers, psychologists studied the generation of categories bottom-up. For example, how do humans learn categories from the basic attributes of objects, which may be independent of, or dependent on, one another [103].

The computing field has studied the methods for codifying ontologies in computer: formal representations of a set of concepts within a domain and the relationships between those concepts. In the Semantic Web area, Web Ontology Language (OWL: https://www.w3.org/standards/techs/owl) was developed for defining and sharing ontologies.

Some existing categories define or interpret dimensions but not every category. For example, a category and its child cannot be two dimensions for the same space. For a society or a smaller community, *it is rational to assume that people can form a consensus on a set of categories, organized in a hierarchical structure.* These categories are the basis for understanding and interpretation.

5.3 Dimension and space

5.3.1 Basic concepts

From the algebra point of view, a dimension is a method for partitioning a set of objects. Different methods for partitioning a set of objects form different dimensions on the set. So a large set of objects can be divided and conquered by appropriately selecting more dimensions. A dimension can also be regarded as a subspace with a specific category of objects and the rules that the objects obey.

Various existing mathematical spaces on texts have been established for efficient operations on texts like information retrieval. In the Vector Space Model [104], each dimension corresponds to a word within text with a weight. A dimension takes non-zero value if a term occurs within the text, otherwise it takes zero value [104,105].

Many models on texts can be viewed as one category of models based on the following assumptions: (1) *Words are independent, and* (2) *one word appearing in different contexts is the same.* The two assumptions are not true from the understanding and interpretation point of views because a different order may render different meanings for the same set of words, and one word appearing in different contexts renders different meanings.

A space can also be a cyber-physical space consisting of cyberspace and physical space. A modern museum can be regarded as a cyber-physical space of multiple dimensions (e.g., *time, region,* and *type*) that define the collections of various types.

In the multi-dimensional Resource Space Model [134], different dimensions represent different categories corresponding to different methods of categorization on the same set of representations. Regarding each categorization method as a dimension forms a multi-dimensional category space, where every point represents a category that has a projection at every dimension. For example, a publication space can include the following dimensions: *subject, time, author,* and *publisher.* The multi-dimensional category space can be normalized to ensure the effectiveness of operations on the space just as the normal forms of the relational database. In a complex multi-dimensional category space, a dimension can be a hierarchy of category and one point can be semantically linked to another point [140,141]. Resources can be located in a space of multiple dimensions such as *time, topic,* and *publication type* (e.g., book, journal, or conference) for efficient retrieval and management.

The multi-dimensional category space has abstraction ability, which enables it to specify big data (e.g., all papers and books of all fields), medium data (e.g., all papers and books of one area), and small data (e.g., one paper). A multi-dimensional category space supports multi-dimensional summarization of any size of representation set.

The subjective view of dimension and the objective view of dimension also indicate a way to verify a mental space by extracting a space from an individual's browsing history and to make recommendations. The dimensions extracted from an individual's reading history reflect an individual's mental space to a certain extent. The common dimensions of the mental spaces of the individuals within a group reflect the common mental space of the group. The common dimensions of the mental spaces of the groups within a community reflect the mental space of a community where members share their mental spaces. Interactions between the individuals of the same group or between the individuals of different groups evolve the groups and therefore evolve the individuals' mental spaces and the groups' mental spaces.

5.3.2 Interest space

An interest space represents interests from multiple dimensions that are independent of each other. Any point has a projection at every dimension. One point can link to another point with a semantic interpretation. A particular interest can be represented as a basic pattern, a semantic link network of points, or a flow through a semantic link network of points.

In cyber-physical-social space, a semantic link will represent the measures (e.g., distance, time, and speed) and rules in the physical space and the measures (e.g., cost and value) and rules in social space. Some rules are for evaluating, predicting and adjusting interests. An interest flow presents and understands complex interests. For readers and writers, an interest flow largely determines a reading process or a writing process. For tourists, an interest flow represents a network of attractions, which reflects the priority and optimization of a travel path considering the types of vehicle (bus, train, taxi, etc.) and the costs of transportation (including time) as shown in Figure 5.3.

Generally, a particular interest representation takes the following form: $<N, L, R, F, CH>$, where N, L, R, F and CH denote the semantic nodes (points in the space), the semantic links between nodes (including physical and social measures), the rules, and the flows through the semantic links, and the category hierarchy that interprets the nodes, semantic links and rules. Different flows can be defined on the same semantic link network.

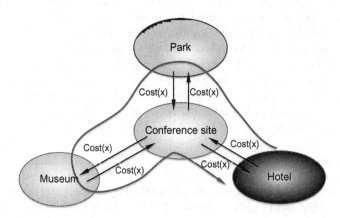

Figure 5.3 An interest flow of tourist. Cost(x) denotes the cost of taking transportation x (taxi, metro, bus, walk).

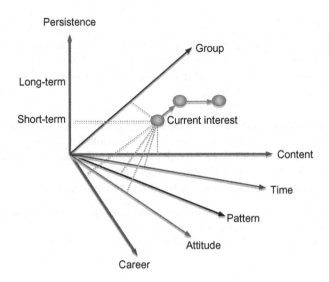

Figure 5.4 A seven-dimensional interest space.

A good content service should satisfy the basic pattern or the flow through a semantic link network of points. The interest flow can be extracted from the order of behaviors such as the clicking flows for browsing web pages and the order of occurrence between the concepts in texts.

Figure 5.4 shows an interest space that consists of the following dimensions: *persistency, user group, content, pattern, attitude,* and *career.* The persistence dimension specifies the short-term interest (disappears quickly) and the long-term interest. The career dimension identifies different stages (*primary school, secondary school, high school for foundation education*) of career development, which can help determine the current interest and estimate future interest, because people at different careers have different interests. Future interest development also depends on the group where the user interacts with the other members of the group. The pattern dimension specifies the types of patterns such as object, link structure and tree structure. The content dimension specifies the category hierarchy of the contents. The attitude dimension represents readers' positive, neutral and negative attitude on the contents. For scientific publications, most researchers take the neutral attitude, but for the other form of text like news and advertisements, many readers have a positive attitude and a negative attitude on some news. So, the attitude dimension is necessary in general. The group dimension specifies different user groups. Different groups have different interests. The current interest is a point in the interest space or a subspace of the interest space.

The fundamental problem of information service is the modeling and maintenance of a multi-dimensional interest space for various users, a multi-dimensional category space for various resources and the mapping from the interest space into the resource space.

5.3.3   Applications

A multi-dimensional space can apply to efficiently managing any types of resources and modeling the interest of various objects including individual user and organization (e.g., company, community and state). The following describes four application scenarios of dimensions and spaces.

Application Scenario 1: A smart online library system can provide services for all types of users, including individual users, organizations (research institutions and enterprises), and strategic services through establishing the multi-dimensional users' mental space, the multi-dimensional resource space, and the mapping between the mental space and the resource space. It has the following features:

1. It manages all library resources through a multi-dimensional category space, which can adapt to the increasing of new resources.
2. It records the users' operations (queries, chats, and clicks for browsing and downloading resources) and the downloaded resources. It discovers the dimensions and the interest semantic link networks on the operations and resources.
3. It builds an interest space for users by recording and analyzing the operations and the contents of downloaded resources and extracting dimensions.
4. It recommends reading resources to the appropriate users according to the matching between the resources and the personal interest space, a subspace of the interest space.
5. The interest space evolves with the continual operations of users, increasing resources, and possible feedbacks (e.g., comments).

Users' interaction with the other systems (including the Internet) influences the evolution of the interest spaces. As the consequence of interaction, the change of their operations incurs the maintenance of the interest model. Figure 5.5 depicts the concept model of the system.

The semantic links between users and between resources support advanced applications, for example:

1. For scientific research, the system can discover the track of science development from the citation network of publications, summarize the existing methods, evaluate research, predict development trend and new research topic, and discover collaborators according to interest and technical requirement. It is also possible to discover the shift of science paradigms through the analysis of historic data.
2. For enterprises, it can discover competitive advantages, the development trend of the technologies and technical solutions, evaluate the status of the company in terms of life-cycle, as well as establish and maintain a supply network to maximize business benefit from big data according to requirement.

Application Scenario 2: A smart website can be designed with the following features:

1. It has a multi-dimensional resource space for storing webpages. Webpages will be stored in and retrieved from a point of the space.
2. It has a collector (crawler) that can collect or create webpages and store them in the multi-dimensional resource space.

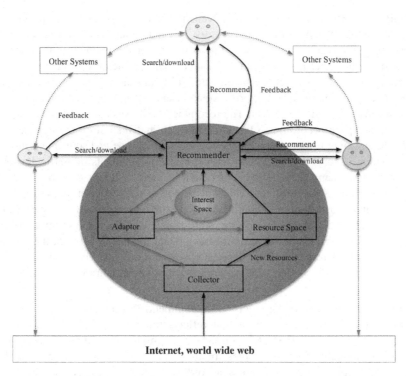

Figure 5.5 A recommendation system model based on the interest space and the resource space.

3. It has a browser that can record users' operations (e.g., clicking links), navigate and display contents.
4. It has a recommender that can recommend the contents according to the resources in the resource space and the users' interest specified by the interest space. It can adapt the dimensions to the change of the interests of users according to the development of the operation history. Summarization carries out to reduce the scale of the contents to be recommended.
5. It generates a multi-dimensional interest space by extracting dimensions from users' operation history and the contents of recommendation.
6. The interest space uses multiple dimensions to hold the interests of all users. It supports the analysis of users' interests, including the distribution and evolution of interests. The analysis result supports the strategies for recommendation based on the adaptive interest space according to change and the estimation of change.
7. It has an adapter that can adapt the resource space, the interest model, the recommendation mechanism and the collector.
8. Different users can read different contents of their own interests. In contrast, the current websites such as Yahoo.com and Sina.com can only display the same content for all users. Current search engines like Google is incorporating users' features like users' locations into queries to get personalized search results.

Application Scenario 3: A mobile content recommendation system can be designed on the basis of the users' interest space incorporating location (determined by GPS and WiFi), the pattern of movement, and the possible user information such as browsing and conversation history. An individual user interest space is a subspace of the whole interest space for all users. For the public, the interests will be more about social dimensions (e.g., events that significantly influence society), economy dimension (e.g., price, income and job), and the psychological dimension (e.g., love, play and health). For professional users, the interests will be more about professional knowledge and data. The recommendation system will collect contents in the cyberspace according to the interest space and then store the contents in a multi-dimensional resource space. Due to the small storage and screen and the long conversation history, it is necessary to summarize the contents on particular topics and then recommend the summarized content to users. The contents to be summarized concern texts, pictures, and videos used during conversation. A dynamic window for capturing the scope of topic is needed. The recommendation system should be able to adjust the dimensions of the interest space and the resource space according to users' feedbacks on the recommendation and the match between the resource space and the interest space. The interest space also provides the basis for recommending appropriate conversation materials such as words, phrases and sentences.

Application Scenario 4: An enterprise recommendation system can be designed on the basis of the interest space that reflects the core business interest of the enterprise. It integrates the collection, analysis, prediction, and summarization of various data, including texts, tables, pictures, and videos. Searching the cyberspace with multiple search engines according to the interest space can collect data. The abstraction ability and the semantic links enable the system to include relevant data. One of the key steps is to discover dimensions, build a multi-dimensional space and use it to store the constantly expanding data. An advanced recommendation system provides multi-dimensional organization of big data for such functions as follows:

1. Finding the causes of the failure of a decision or a product. The basis of the solution is to find the cause-effect links in the data.
2. Predicting the behaviors of suppliers and customers, and therefore enhancing the bargain power.
3. Finding the pattern of customers and therefore planning the supply chain to minimize the cost of storage and delivery.
4. Evaluating the potential risks and competitive advantages.
5. Determining frauds information.
6. Finding new opportunities, including new market, new product, new customers and new suppliers.

In general, *the challenge problem of information service is automatically constructing and maintaining a multi-dimensional interest space for various subjects, a multi-dimensional category space for efficiently managing various objects, and the mapping from the interest space into the space of objects.* The background is the Cyber-Physical Society, where subjects live, work, create, study, communicate and manage to generate and evolve interests and objects.

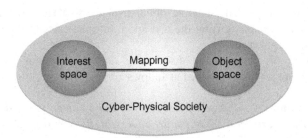

Figure 5.6 The general solution to the fundamental problem of information services. The Cyber-Physical Society determines the motivation, value and policy for the organization of the interest space and the object space.

Figure 5.6 depicts the general solution to the fundamental problem of information service.

5.4 Discovering dimensions

This section presents an empirical method for discovering dimensions in a given set of general resources. The empirical rationale will be interpreted by text applications. The theoretical basis is the Resource Space Model [134,141]. To keep consistency with the Resource Space Model, the word "resource" is used to represent "object" in the following discussion.

5.4.1 Problem definition

Discovering dimensions involves in three parts: *dimension in mind* (subjective), *pattern in resources* (objective), and *mapping between the dimension in mind and the pattern in resources*. The change of the resources may change the pattern in resources and then may influence the dimension in mind. Discovering dimensions in resources is to find the mapping between the dimensions in minds and the patterns in resources.

The problem is that it is difficult to completely define all dimensions in minds. A rational assumption is that research result is for use by a group of people, and there exists a high-level category hierarchy, which has been agreed to by all people within the group.

Online category hierarchies reflect the dimensions in minds of many contributors, so the above assumption is rational. These category hierarchies can help automatically discover dimensions as pointed out in [141].

Texts are resources that contain rich patterns. There are two purposes of the efforts to represent text: *Retrieval* and *Understanding*. For retrieval, features like term frequency of texts are tractable and easy for match-making in principle. For understanding, features with term frequency are at a very low level, which do not support understanding. Understanding often involves a category hierarchy that is beyond text, and a mapping from the text space into the category hierarchy representing people's consensus.

The problem of automatically discovering dimension within a given set of resources (e.g., texts) can be defined as follows:

Problem definition: *Given a set of resources R and a category hierarchy CH, find a set of criteria to extract a set of feature representations W from R, and then find a category tree CT within CH according to W such that R can be classified by CT.*

Figure 5.7 depicts the problem of discovering dimensions within a given set of resources. The key problem is how to find the rules or criteria to extract the feature representations W (patterns) in resources, select a category tree CT from CH by matching the pattern in resources and the patterns in categories, and use CT to classify resources. However, it is difficult in many cases to find the rules for accurately extracting the patterns in various resources. An empirical solution is to find some indicators to indicate patterns. For example, we can find some representation units (like words) in texts to indicate the patterns in texts.

In an open society, the category hierarchy CH evolves with the evolution of society, and the set of resources evolves with the changes of requirements, applications and human behaviors; therefore the patterns of the resources change, as the consequence, the category tree CT changes, and finally the organization of resources with dimensions changes.

The problem can be broken down into several sub-problems, which will be discussed in the following sections. In the following discussion, $X(C_1, \ldots, C_m)$ indicates a dimension, $C_1, \ldots,$ and C_m indicates the coordinates (subcategories) of X,

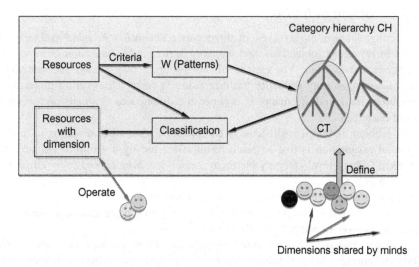

Figure 5.7 The problem of discovering a dimension. The rectangle represents the boundary of the automatic system.

and W is used to represent the set of indicators extracted from resources to render the patterns in the resources.

5.4.2   Category space

Category space consists of categories and various relations between categories. Current category representation uses name and hierarchical structure to represent the relations between categories. However, the names of categories and the structure of the category hierarchy are not enough to represent the semantics of the category hierarchy.

From rationalism, it is hard to accurately define the large-scale categories, which can interpret the subjective aspects. Formalization helps make provable interpretation but in this case formalism may be either too general (like graph theory) or too basic (like the Vector Space Model) to guide real applications.

From empiricism, it is feasible to construct the category hierarchy by making use of the current online category hierarchies like the category network of Wikipedia. The advantages of using Wikipedia include the following three points: (1) the populations of users, (2) each category has a page that makes informal interpretation and the page can evolve with the evolution of cognition of contributors, and (3) it has a network of categories although it may need some adjustments.

The problem is that the online categories like in Wikipedia are too general to suit particular applications. The following are two solutions:

1. *Automatic solution. Extend the existing categories to meet the need of particular applications by designing an automatic process.*
2. *Hybrid solution. Build an evolving system to collect the requirements on new categories, and identify appropriate people who can be encouraged to define new categories.*

To reflect multi-dimensional views of humans, an n-dimensional category space is necessary to specify and organize categories, represented as follows: $CS(d_1$: *pattern*$_1$, ..., d_n: *pattern*$_n$), where d_k: *pattern*$_k$ represents the name of dimension k and the pattern on the dimension. As shown in Figure 5.8, a category in the category space is a point defined by (d_1: *pattern*$_1(C)$, ..., d_n: *pattern*$_n(C)$), where d_k: *pattern*$_k(C)$ represents the pattern of category C at dimension d_k, $1 \leq k \leq n$. For the categories about science in Wikipedia, the dimensions include *definition*,

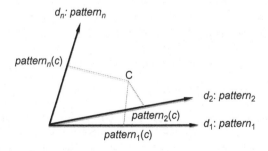

Figure 5.8 A multi-dimensional category space.

history, *philosophy*, and *theory*, and each dimension is defined by a natural language representation, which contains a pattern of words.

A category tree consists of a set of categories selected from the category space and the subcategory relations, represented as $CT = (\{C_1(p_1), \ldots, C_n(p_n)\}, \leq)$, where $\leq$ denotes the subcategory relation between categories, and the pattern of a category is the generalization of the patterns of its children, reflecting the common characteristics. With the category tree, it is not difficult to solve the following problem:

Problem definition: *Given a category tree CT and a set of resources (e.g., texts) R, use CT to classify R so that resources can be managed (e.g., retrieved) efficiently.*

As the result of classification, each category can represent a subset of resources.

5.4.3 Resource space

Using the category tree to classify a set of resources generates a one-dimensional resource space, where each category represents a set of resources R sharing a pattern P. A category in the resource space is defined by the following three elements:

1. A set of resources R.
2. The pattern of the resources P_r.
3. The pattern defined in the category P_c.

Therefore, a category can be represented as $C(R, P_r, P_c)$.

The purpose of defining two patterns is to distinguish the dynamicity of the resources from the dynamicity of human cognition. The pattern of the resources evolves with the change of resources, which may be prominent in some applications and stable in some other applications. The pattern defining the category evolves with human cognition. For the applications on resource management, if the evolution of the category (e.g., ACM CCS) is much slower than the change of resources, it can be used as a criterion to evaluate the change of the category of resources, for example, when resources increase constantly. For the applications of category definition, if the evolution of resources is much slower than the change of the categories, the categories of resources can be used as a criterion to evaluate the change of the category, for example, when developing new categories.

A one-dimensional Resource Space RS is a partial order on a category set such that: if the categories on resources satisfy a partial order denoted as $\leq$, then the resources belonging to them also satisfy a partial order. RS is represented as RS $(R, \{C_1, \ldots, C_n\}, \leq, \subseteq)$, where R denotes resource set, $\{C_1, \ldots, C_n\}$ denotes a set of categories, and $\subseteq$ denotes the inclusion relation between resource sets, and satisfies:

1. If $C_i \leq C_j$ (C_i is more special than C_j) then $R_i \subseteq R_j$, where R_i and R_j are subset of R and belong to C_i and C_j respectively.
2. For all children $C_1, \ldots,$ and C_k of a category C, $R = R_1 \cup \ldots \cup R_k$ holds, where $R_1, \ldots,$ and R_k belong to $C_1, \ldots,$ and C_k respectively and R belongs to category C.
3. Any two children C_l and C_m of the same category have no common resources, i.e., $R_l \cap R_m = \varnothing$.

5.4.4 Mutual-reference adaption

Humans created various resources such as texts, images and data about human. Humans also designed various devices to capture data of various natural or artificial systems. There are some relations between the resource space and human mental space.

At the beginning when there is no resource in the resource management system, the patterns that define the categories in the category hierarchy (CH) are the only criterion to select resources. When the system contains more and more resources, the selection of resources should consider both the pattern of categories in the category hierarchy and the pattern of the resources in the resource space. Uploading a resource into the appropriate point depends on the matching between the pattern of the resource and the patterns of the categories of the category hierarchy.

A problem will arise when the current resource categories are not suitable for specifying the new resources. The resource space can adapt to change through the following three operations:

1. Add a new resource category as a child to an appropriate category.
2. Split one resource category C into two categories as the children of C.
3. Merge two resource categories as one category of the same parent.

The category tree will be the criteria for judging the rationality of the operations, with the assumption that the category tree is relatively stable.

When the resource management system contains a big volume of resources, the patterns of the resource category reflect the patterns in the mental space, and therefore become the criteria for evaluating the adaption of the category tree when it is significantly different from the categories of resources or when some people want to update it.

5.4.5 Assumption

As strings, words are not able to interpret themselves. Words are interpreted when they are mapped into the mental categories. One word appearing in different contexts may be mapped into different categories so it gets different interpretations. It is the same for the other forms of representations.

As it is difficult to define mental categories, people often use a set of common representations (e.g., standards) to interpret new representations. Experienced people are also able to generalize rules and criteria from the agreed representations to help other people to reach consensus on new representations. This is the way for a community to make an interpretable space of representations. This gives the rational and motivation to automatically find the criteria for extracting appropriate representations from resources.

The following assumption is to identify the representation components within each resource of the observed resource set. It assumes that the representation of a resource can be decomposed into several representation components. For example, word and sentence can be identified within text. This is the basis for discovering dimensions on the given resource set.

Assumption 1: There exists a set of rules or a set of criteria that can extract representation components within the observed resource.

For automatically discovering the indicators of dimensions in resources, existing categories like the categories of Wikipedia can be used to interpret a representation.

Assumption 2: A representation is interpretable if it can be mapped into a category hierarchy agreed by the observers.

For example, it is rationale to regard the word as interpretable if a word can be mapped into the existing category hierarchy. The interpretability of representation is the basis of the interpretability of the representations used to indicate dimensions.

Assumption 3: There exists a mapping from a representation in the observed resources into the existing category hierarchy, and the more general category and the more special category are available from that category.

Once the dimensions of a given set of texts are found, the dimensions can provide more accurate content services in such applications as multi-dimensional recommendation, summarization and question answering.

5.4.6 Criteria

Criteria help select candidate representations to indicate dimensions or co-ordinates (sub-categories) on a given set of resources.

The first criterion requests the representativeness of the representation in all resources because a dimension needs to specify all resources of the given set of resources. A representation that appears or appears in a more special form in all resources can be an index for accessing all resources.

In-All Criterion: For a given set of resources, if a representation or its specialization appears in all resources, it is a candidate representation that indicates a dimension on the set of resources.

For example, a word commonly used by all authors of the given set of texts is likely to indicate a common view, so it is reasonable to select it as a candidate indicator of a dimension. However, many representations (e.g., words) may appear in all resources (e.g., texts); for example, some words such as "the," "a," "of," and "to" frequently appearing in every text should not be selected as a candidate indicator. The following criterion is needed to exclude these trivial representations.

Minimum Criterion: *For a given set of resources, if a representation or its specialization appears the minimum times in every resource, it is a candidate representation indicating a dimension on the set of resources.*

In other words, if w and w' are candidate indicators but w' appears more times in resources r_1, ..., and r_n than w, then w takes the priority to be selected. For selecting a set of candidate indicators, this criterion is to select the top-k indicators that appear the minimum times in all resources.

The minimum criterion requests the representativeness of a candidate criterion. The basic rationale concerns the following aspects:

1. *The representations appeared the minimum times in every resource can distinguish themselves from those frequently appeared representations.*
2. *The representations appeared the minimum times in every resource can represent common view as they appear in every resource.*
3. *The minimum appeared representation resembles one extreme among all representations.*

Take texts for example, the words appeared the minimum times resemble a different extreme from the extreme identified by frequently appeared terms. This criterion can select the representations that appear just one time such as *author* and *publication time* and the representations that represent the core, which also normally appeared just one time.

The following are observations that support the above two criteria.

Observation 1: In cyberspace, the time of generating resources (e.g., publishing texts, taking pictures, etc.) is recorded in the digital resources so time can be a dimension of all digital resources. In most cases, the word "time" may not appear in text. The word "time" is the generalization of the special representation such as 23/05/2016 and 23 May 2016.

Observation 2: In Wikipedia, "history" appears in all pages that introduce research areas, so "history" can be a dimension of these pages. A definition sentence appears at the beginning of every page although the word definition does not appear. The location is an implicit representation that indicates the definition in every Wikipedia page.

Observation 3: Taking news for example, the above two criteria can find the candidate indicators of dimensions such as "location" and "time" because they appeared in all news (otherwise readers don't know where and when the event happens) with the least time (it is not necessary to mention the location and the time of a happened event multiple times). If the news is about people, people also satisfy the above two criteria.

Observation 4: Taking papers for example, *publication time, publisher, journal, author, introduction, affiliation,* and *References* satisfy the above two criteria because they appeared in all papers and appeared just one time.

However, the representations indicating the core of the resource may not appear the minimum times or the maximum times. The weight of representation, the weight of component and the weight of relation are three indicators of the core.

Usually, the words in the title, in the caption of pictures and in the tables indicate the core better than the other parts of the text. In scientific papers, the words appearing in the title, keyword list, abstract, introduction section, caption of figures and tables, and conclusion section indicate the core. In addition to the locations of representations, the words appearing in the important relations like cause-effect are often relevant to the core because these words represent the authors' thinking and the authors' need to spend more time to represent them than other simple sentences. My student Menyun Cao and I conducted a survey on the role of the cause-effect relation in scientific papers. The result shows that about 80% of words in the abstracts appear in the cause-effect sentences of papers. The following criterion deals with this case.

Core Criterion: For a set of resources, *if a representation or its specialization indicates the core of every resource, it is a candidate representation indicating a dimension on the set of resources.*

The core criterion selects the representations that indicate the main view on a given set of resources. Take texts for example, one piece of text usually has just one core. Most words are used to render the core. This is one extreme people often used: *the maximum extreme,* which is heavily represented by many words. The other extreme is *the minimum extreme,* which is lightly represented by one phrase. The minimum extreme is rendered by the indicators selected by the minimum-criterion. In some cases, the maximum extreme and the minimum extreme converge into one, for example, a short text like a sentence or a paragraph.

For texts, the abstract word like "country" usually indicates a category of countries while the specific word like "China" usually indicates a specific country. For the same reason, "author" can be a candidate indicator while author name like "Hai Zhuge" should not be a candidate indicator of a dimension. The in-all criterion and the minimum criterion include the case that the representation appears in a specialization form in resources. The following criterion deals with this case.

Abstraction Criterion: If w and w' are two candidate representations that indicate a dimension and w is more abstract than w', then w takes the priority to be selected.

This criterion requests a candidate representation for indicating a dimension to be an abstract representation. A more abstract representation can cover more resources. The abstraction level depends on the satisfactory of other criteria, for example, the independency between sub-categories (coordinates).

Take texts for example, if "Jackie Chan" appears in one part of news, and "Jet Li" appears in the other part of the news, and both can be mapped into the category "actor" within the existing category hierarchy, then the "actor" can be a candidate dimension with two coordinates: "Jackie Chan" and "Jet Li", denoted as *actor (Jackie Chan, Jet Li)*, although "actor" does not appear in text. If "China", "Japan", and "USA" appearing in a set of news can be mapped into a category "country" within existing category hierarchy, "country" can be a dimension, denoted as

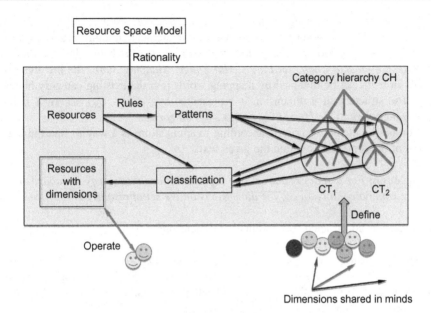

Figure 5.9 The problem of discovering multiple dimensions.

country (*China, Japan, USA*). The identification of names within texts is necessary for automation, which has been studied in natural language processing area.

Figure 5.9 depicts the problem of discovering multiple dimensions.

A good dimension should be independent of the other dimensions of the same
space, otherwise it does not help clearly divide the resources in the space for efficiently
operating the resources. It is difficult to determine the independence between representations without mapping into the existing categories. Some empirical criteria based on
common sense can be given. Take texts for example, the hierarchies of dimensions
should not have duplicate words, synonyms, closely related words, etc. For example,
"apple" and "fruit" (and "artificial intelligence" and "knowledge representation")
should not be two dimensions in the same space. The distance between representations
can be measured by defining the distance between the categories they indicated.

Independence Criterion: *The candidate representations should be independent of
each other, i.e., the interpretation of one candidate representation is neither the
parent nor the ancestor of the interpretation of another.*

As the consequence of the above criterion, we have the following constructive
criterion.

Tree Criterion: *A good candidate indicator of a dimension takes a tree structure,
which can be interpreted by a category tree such that each category interprets a
candidate indicator.*

This is because a category tree can divide a large resource set at different abstraction levels. A good dimension takes a hierarchical structure. Take texts for example, the dimension *people (actor, professor, student)* is better than the dimension *people (Jackie Chan, Jet Li, . . ., Hai Zhuge, Xiaoping Sun)*. The hierarchy of words in texts can be obtained by mapping words into the existing category hierarchy. The structure of a dimension is represented as $X(C_1,. . .,C_m)$, *where X is the root category and C_1, . . ., and C_m are its sub-categories.*

Combining the above criteria according to applications is a way to find the indicators of the dimensions within the given texts.

Proposition: *For a set of resources, the representations that satisfy the above criteria are rationale indicators of the dimensions on the set of resources.*

A space is constructed by coordinating dimensions.

Space Criterion: *Given the structure of a dimension $X(C_1, . . ., C_m)$, construct another dimension $X'(C_1', . . ., C_n')$ such that $R(X(C_i)) = R(X'(C_i'))$, where $R(X(C_i))$ and $R(X'(C_j'))$ represent the resources indicated by coordinates C_i and C_j' respectively, and $1 \le i \le m$ and $1 \le j \le n$.*

Extracting the patterns from the given representations is the basis for obtaining the pattern of the definitions of categories, the patterns of the representations of resources, and the patterns of different representations of the resources. These patterns are the basis for mapping resources into categories. For applications on texts, if words are regarded as representation components, the problem can be solved by many existing technologies, e.g., the vector space model and topic model, which are suitable for retrieving texts. But these models cannot interpret the mapping from words into category. If representation components include phrase, sentence and paragraph, the pattern of phrases and the patterns of sentences should be known. Based on these patterns, the mapping from those patterns into the patterns of the existing categories can be established.

All dimensions of a resource space need to satisfy some criteria, otherwise dimensions are separate. The basic criterion is that a point has projections at every dimension.

Resource Space Criterion: *For any pair of dimensions $X(C_1, . . ., C_m)$ and $X'(C_1', . . ., C_n')$ in the space, $R(X(C_i)) = R(X'(C_j'))$ holds, where $R(X(C_i))$ and $R(X'(C_j'))$ represent the resources indicated by coordinates C_i and C_j' respectively, and $1 \le i \le m$ and $1 \le j \le n$.*

5.4.7 Extending dimension

There are two cases that need to extend an existing dimension: (1) the initial dimensions of the resource space no longer suit the current application requirement (e.g., the new resources cannot find an appropriate category), and (2) the category hierarchy is too general to be used for constructing the resource space for domain applications. The first case requires the extension of the dimensions of a resource space. The second case requires the extension of the category hierarchy. The following is the common problem:

Problem: *Given the structure of a dimension $X(C_1, \ldots, C_n)$, expand each subcategories (coordinates) $C_1, \ldots,$ and C_n into a tree structure such that the children of the same node are independent of each other.*

The category indicated by $X(C_1, \ldots, C_n)$ limits the sub-categories under $C_1, \ldots,$ and C_n. The terminate condition can be the height and the width of the trees, the balanced distribution of resources in categories, search efficiency, and a category level that matches users' interest.

Solutions to the above problems can enforce each other. Solving the first problem needs to extend the resource space according to the patterns of the current resources, the patterns of new requirements, and the existing category hierarchy. Solving the second problem needs to extend the category hierarchy by specializing the current categories according to the patterns in the current resources and the patterns of new requirements.

To extend multiple dimensions of a space needs a little more work because the extension to every dimension needs to coordinate with each other to ensure that the extended dimensions construct a space.

5.4.8 Automatic construction

There are three parties that participate in automatic construction of resource space: a set of resources, a hierarchy of categories and users. The following are categories of the problem:

1. *Resource-oriented construction, i.e., constructing a resource space according to a set of resources and a hierarchy of categories.* This concerns two cases of the set of resources: relatively stable, and quickly changing. For the first case, the key is to discover the patterns within the set of resources, and map the patterns into the category hierarchy to construct the category tree. For the second case, if change is predictable, the change of the pattern of the resource set is predictable, then the key to solution is to adjust the space according to the prediction on the change of the pattern. If the change is unpredictable, the solution has to adjust the space when the pattern of the resource set changes prominently. Therefore, the problem in this case becomes the first case. So this section just discusses the case where the patterns of the resource set are stable.

2. *Application-oriented construction, i.e., constructing a resource space according to application requirement.* This requests the description of the requirement, for example, implicit interests and explicit query requirements. For explicit query requirement, the problem becomes how to extract the patterns from the query requirements and construct the category trees by mapping the patterns into the categories in the category hierarchy.

For the implicit interest, a new problem emerges: how to automatically extract user interests? One way is to extract user interests from users' operation history (e.g., clicking history for browsing Web). So the condition consists of the following three parts:
a. *Operation history.*
b. *Resources to be managed.*
c. *Category hierarchy.*

A basic construction problem is to construct a new dimension according to a given dimension such that the two dimensions construct a resource space. In real applications like text summarization, there often exists a main dimension, e.g., the dimension constructed by the core criterion. The main dimension can be used as a reference for constructing other dimensions because all dimensions of a resource space need to specify the same set of resources. The problem is to find other dimensions according to this main dimension. Generally, dimensions can be weighted according to the requirements of different applications. The problem is stated as follows:

Problem: *Given a set of resources, a category hierarchy and a dimension $X(C_1, \ldots, C_m)$, construct another dimension $X'(C_1', \ldots, C_n')$ such that $R(X(C_i)) = R(X'(C_j'))$, where $R(X(C_i))$ and $R(X'(C_j'))$ represent the resources indicated by coordinates C_i and C_j' respectively, and $1 \leq i \leq m$ and $1 \leq j \leq n$.*

The above problem can be extended to construct k dimensions as follows.

Problem: *Given a set of resources and a category hierarchy, construct a space consisting of k dimensions such that for any two dimensions $X(C_1, \ldots, C_m)$ and $X'(C_1', \ldots, C_n')$, $R(X(C_i)) = R(X'(C_j'))$ holds, where $1 \leq i \leq m$ and $1 \leq j \leq n$.*

The following are several relevant problems for discovering dimensions and constructing space.

1. *Given a set of resources, a category hierarchy and the name of one dimension, construct a dimension.*
2. *Given a set of resources, a category hierarchy and the names of k dimensions, construct a k-dimensional resource space.*
3. *Given a set of resources and a category hierarchy, construct a k-dimensional resource space.*

5.4.9 Automatically uploading resources

After the construction of resource space, uploading resources into resources space is an important part of the applications of the Resource Space Model. There are two ways to upload resources into resource space: one is manual and the other is automatic. Manual uploading resources into resource space relies on human understanding of the resource space and the resources. Automatically uploading resources into resource space is a part of automation of resource space.

There are two criteria for an uploading mechanism to determine which point a resource needs to be uploaded:

1. *The interpretation of dimensions.* A dimension is interpreted by the patterns of the category tree that define the structure of the dimension. A new resource can be put into the point if the general pattern of the category trees of the dimensions that define a point matches the pattern in the new resource.
2. *The existing resources in the point.* A new resource can be put into the point if the pattern in the resources of a point matches the pattern in the new resource.

At the beginning when there are few resources in the points, the uploading mechanism needs to use the first criteria. When there are many resources in the points, the uploading mechanism needs to consider both criteria.

5.4.10 Discovering dimensions on the network of resources

Previous discussion regards resources as a set. Links between resources are neglected. In many cases, resources are linked, in one form or the other, closely or loosely. One resource can work for one task or for multiple tasks. A network of resources can work together for one task or for multiple tasks.

The problem of discovering dimensions on the network of resources can be described as follows:

Given a network of resources and a category hierarchy, discover a k-dimensional resource space such that the management (e.g., search) of the network is more efficient.

The traditional approaches to discovering the communities of a network can only discover one dimension—the hierarchy of communities.

Take research papers for example, citations connect papers, and papers within one area are closely related. The problem will be specialized as: *Given a citation network of papers and a category hierarchy, discover a k-dimensional resource space such that the management of the network of papers is more efficient.*

The typical operations of the papers include finding all or the latest papers of a given area (represented by the main dimension), finding all, all papers on a particular topic, or the latest papers of a given author, and finding all or the latest papers published in a particular journal, and finding all collaborators of a given author. These queries need the dimensions on *area, time, publisher,* and *author,* which are neglected by traditional classification methods.

The following are two solutions to solve the above problems:

1. Discover k dimensions on the resources first as discussed in previous sections, and then use the community discovery approaches to discover one more dimension on the network, and finally construct a $k+1$ dimensional resource space. This space provides more accurate and quick access to resources. For example, in the citation network of research papers, k dimensions can be discovered on papers, and one dimension can be discovered from the citation network, and therefore a $k+1$ dimensional paper space can be constructed for efficient access to the contents of papers.

2. Discover the communities to construct one dimension, then find the k common dimensions within each community, and finally generate a $k + 1$ dimensional space. This space provides more accurate access to communities. For example, in the citation network of research papers, research areas can be discovered from the papers first, and then discover k common dimensions within the communities, and finally generate a $k + 1$ dimensional paper space for efficient access to the communities of papers (research areas).

A more general problem is: *given a semantic link network of resources and a category hierarchy, construct a k-dimensional resource space such that the management of the network is more efficient.* Typical management operations include searching specific relations, node or pattern according to a given condition.

The solution to the above problem can apply to discover a multi-dimensional space on the network of various resources (buildings, people, cars, etc.) of cities.

5.5 The space of methodologies

Different streams of methodologies are based on different worldviews; for example, rationalism believes that the meaning of text is determined by its structure and derivation rules. The principles underlying the structure of language are biologically determined by human minds and genetically transmitted. Humans share the same underlying linguistic structure [20,21]. Social constructivism believes that any text is involved in society (e.g., in power relationships) and history [40,41]. Evolutionism concerns the process of mental development and innate mental structures [113].

In category hierarchy, a category is more general than its sub-categories and represents more objects than any of its subcategories. Independent high-level categories of methodologies can be regarded as different dimensions of a methodology space such that each point specifies one methodology or a group of methodologies that are closely related to each other and has a projection on every dimension. Figure 5.10 depicts a multi-dimensional methodology space consisting of the following main dimensions [141]:

1. *Empiricism.* A high-level category of methodologies believes knowledge comes from experience and emphasizes evidence, especially data sensed through equipment or derived from experiment. It assumes that knowledge (including concepts, methods, theories, ..., etc.) is convincible and reliable, at least within a certain scope.
2. *Evolutionism.* A high-level category of methodologies believes complex systems or species develop through evolution. Summaries should be able to evolve with various interactions in the complex space like the evolution of the Wikipedia. Writers, readers and languages evolve and influence each other while co-evolving.
3. *Individual and social constructionism.* A high-level category of methodologies believes that meaning and understanding develop with individuals and society. For summarization, writing and reading involve both individual thinking and social experience and interaction.

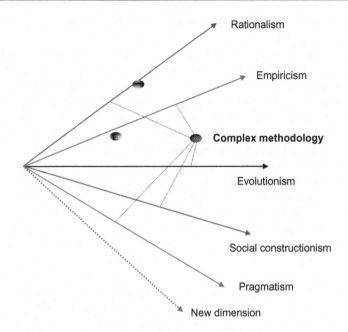

Figure 5.10 A multi-dimensional methodological space.

4. *Rationalism.* A high-level category of methodologies regards reasoning as the main source of knowledge. Rational study derives new theories and methods according to existing theories, methods and phenomena.

5. *Pragmatism.* A high-level category of methodologies believes that knowledge comes from practical use. Research should be useful and benefit human life and social development. Solving the problems emerged in practice provides instances for rational thinking and verification.

Each dimension can have many coordinates, each of which is a tree of categories. Distance between methodologies can be defined according to the distance at every dimension such that close methodologies are organized in the same subspace. A distinguished new methodology needs to be specified by creating a new point with two operations: (1) adding new categories to each dimension, and (2) maintaining the existing dimension according to the criteria of the space.

Creating a dimension is to create a new high-level category of methodology, which is a revolution of the methodology space because the relations between the existing dimensions and the new dimensions need to be assessed and all methodologies in the space need to be assessed and mapped onto this new dimension.

The methodology space provides a coordinate system for managing, analyzing, comparing, and evaluating methodologies and inspiring the creation of new methodologies. For example, the difference between two methodologies can be compared from different dimensions in the space. New methodologies can be assessed and then put into an appropriate point in the space. This methodological space can help examine the nature of a methodology from multiple dimensions and the position at each dimension.

Many phenomena have shown that what a person (especially a child) learns about the world is based on an innate mental structure [72,73]. The innate mental structure includes more than Chomsky's universal grammar of linguistic structure. The cyberspace, physical space and social space have structures, and the brains have evolved along the ways to recognize and represent these structures and the structure of themselves. From the evolutionism point of view, this structure evolves with the development of human beings (biological characteristics and social characteristics) and the development of language.

The difference between the understandings of human beings and the understanding of other beings indicates the difference between the mental structure of humans and the mental structure of other beings. Understanding relies on the information processing mechanism and knowledge processing mechanism in the mind. Methods are limited in their inventors' knowledge and understandings of problems. Integrating different methods is a way to break the limitations.

Big data creates a new methodology based on data exploration. By comparing its main method with existing dimensions, the methodology can be mapped onto the empiricism dimension and the pragmatism dimension. It could become a new dimension when it develops a new method that is different from the existing methodologies belonging to the empiricism dimension and the pragmatism dimension.

5.6 Summary

This chapter mainly answers the following questions: What is dimension? How to discover dimensions? What is the relationship between the dimensions of the resource space and the dimensions of the mental space? How to automatically construct and adapt a multi-dimensional space? A multi-dimensional resource space provides multi-dimensional perspectives for efficiently and effectively understanding and managing resources—various data, methods, and methodologies. Multidimensional methodology provides various methodologies for managing, coordinating, mapping, and composing methodologies as well as guiding applications and predicting the development methodologies.

Characteristics and principles of understanding and representation

As a kind of language representation process, summarization is based on some basic principles of language use and understanding. Observing and rethinking the basic characteristics of language use and understanding can inspire research on summarization as language use and understanding concern the way of observation, experience, communication, thinking, and representation.

6.1 The level of representation

Human representation mainly concerns three levels: physical representation (including data representation), information representation, and knowledge representation as depicted on the left-hand side of Figure 6.1. The information representation, generated from sensing and modeling the physical representation, bridges the physical representation and the knowledge representation.

Building intelligent systems in cyberspace concerns four-level representations as depicted on the right-hand side of Figure 6.1. The language representation refers to the use of various languages to represent data through various ways of observation, it has a certain structure like the format of a scientific paper, which facilitates representation and understanding. The structure of representation components helps human reading and understanding. An information representation is generated through reading the language representation with the knowledge of language use and understanding. The semantic link network of concepts (a basic structure of the semantic image [139]) renders the semantics that the language units indicate. The semantic link network of concepts can guide the summarization of language representation. The knowledge representation in cyberspace is based on the semantic link network of concepts, which interprets language representation and information representation. Mapping between different representations is the basis for automatic language use and understanding.

6.2 The core

Summarization is a mapping from the original representation into a representation that satisfies a certain volume and content constrains.

A mapping is called a summarization only when it reduces the volume of the original representation and ensures that the core of the output representation

Multi-Dimensional Summarization in Cyber-Physical Society. DOI: http://dx.doi.org/10.1016/B978-0-12-803455-2.00006-8

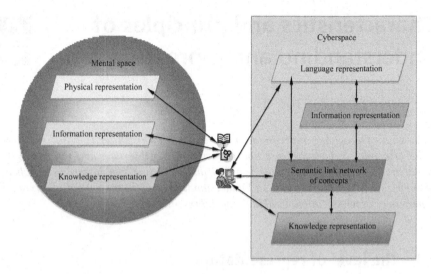

Figure 6.1 Many problems can be regarded as the mappings between representations of different levels.

(summary) is the same as or close to the core of the original text or an integral component of the original text.

It is rational to assume that the representation for summarization is a complete component of human representation (e.g., a section of a paper) as this assumption concerns almost all real requirements and provides a more meaningful input for summarization (it becomes a different problem if the input representation is incomplete). It is also rational to link human representations to their cores because humans write with certain motivation—the mental operation that stimulates, promotes, and controls actions toward a goal. Human motivation can be defined in a multi-dimensional space. Maslow gave the following two dimensions: (1) *Aspiration*, including goal, environment, social link, collaboration, and the sense of accomplishment, (2) *Need*, including physiological, safety, love, esteem, and self-actualization [71].

The core of a representation reflects the conception of the author's thought or emotion based on motivation. For most scientific research, goal, sense of accomplishment, esteem, and self-actualization can be the general motivation, which can be divided into some specific motivations such as solving problems, interpreting new phenomena and reporting new discovery.

Although the representation of summary and the representation of the original text may be different, they should share the same core. A core can be regarded as a semantic link network of concepts that are indicated by representation and led by motivation. For scientific papers, the patterns as in abstracts render the general core, which can guide and evaluate summarization.

Figure 6.2 depicts the triangle of motivation space, category space and language representation space. Motivation leads the mapping between the language representation

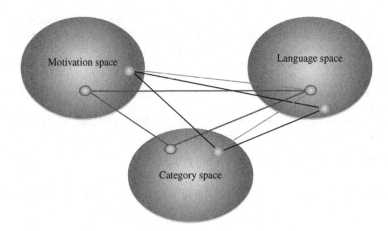

Figure 6.2 Triangle of motivation, category and language representation.

space and the category space. One motivation can be mapped into different language representations, and different motivations can be mapped into one-language representations. A language representation can be mapped into different cores in the category space with different motivations, and different language representations can be mapped into one core in the category space with the same motivation.

Consistency is a criterion of evaluating a general summarization. The distance between the motivation of summarization and the motivation of the original text determine the distance between their cores. For query-based summarization, the motivation of summarization is represented in the query.

6.3 Characteristics, principles and strategies

The following are the basic characteristics of language use and understanding.

1. *Independency-connectivity duality. One of the natural characteristics of human being is both individual independency and connectivity.* Individuals are created independently, the internal systems of individuals like human circulation systems cannot connect one another directly to form a bigger system, and human minds cannot directly access each other either. This independency is a basic principle that forms diversity and various structures in society. From the system point of view, this individual independency is a kind of isolation, localization or encapsulation of components of a system (e.g., in object-oriented methodology) to simplify the structure of the system. Zooming out, every individual links to a group of individuals (following different principles like the small-world principle) and a certain amount of resources to ensure its development. For language use and understanding, on one hand, individuals use and understand language independently; on the other hand, individuals communicate with each other to establish common sense and develop language.

2. *Human host. Humans create and use languages to realize indirect communication between minds.* Communication enables humans to share knowledge and form communities.

3. *Knowledge in minds evolves and self-organizes through language use and understanding.*

4. *The use and understanding of language relies on knowledge.* The use of language needs the knowledge of language, and the understanding of language needs not only the knowledge of language but also the knowledge about the content, common sense and domain knowledge.

5. *The representation of knowledge is not unique.* Knowledge can be represented in natural language, mathematics and other forms.

6. *The understanding of representation is not unique.* This is because of the diversity of representation and differences of knowledge in minds.

These characteristics lead to the following principles:

Separation Principle: The following three kinds of separations are involved in language:

1. *Structure (grammar) and semantics are separated.* Semantics cannot be directly derived from structure. It is clear that sentences of the same structure often represent different meanings. Actually, people do not rely on grammar in oral communication.

2. *Knowledge for representation* (e.g., grammars and idioms) *and knowledge to be represented (e.g., scientific knowledge) are separated.* An example is that researchers have difficulty in writing a scientific paper if they lack either knowledge of language or scientific knowledge.

3. *Representation and its summarization are separated.* It is clear that the process of writing the original text takes place before writing its summary. This leads to the separation of author's meaning and reader's understanding, which is involved in the summarization process.

The above separation principles lead to the natural obstacle of summarization.

In cyberspace, the problem of designing a suitable summarizer can be transformed into the problem of searching for a suitable summarizer. This becomes more feasible with the rapid development of open sources.

A structure on individuals forms and evolves with constant social interaction and selection. The suitable summarizer for summarizing a representation is rendered through the evolution of the semantic link network consisting of writers, readers and various representations.

The social selection concerns motivation, requirement, economy and culture of the society. Social selection selects not only people but also knowledge.

Knowledge Selection Principle: *Knowledge is formed, confirmed, used and propagated through a semantic link network with social selection. The person who shares the represented knowledge (e.g., scientific knowledge, common sense) and the knowledge for representation (knowledge of language) is suitable for summarization, which is a process of using knowledge.*

The above principle means that even people sharing the represented knowledge may not be the suitable person for summarizing the representation because they may not have the knowledge of representation. A friend of an author may not be the suitable summarizer. Knowledge selection concerns the knowledge structure of individuals in addition to the mentioned aspects of the social selection. The suitable person should have similar experience with the author (including education, work, etc.) through which knowledge is generated and confirmed.

Additivity: *A representation is understandable if all of its components are understandable and linked in an understandable way.*

There is a space of studying the links between sentences and between paragraphs because there is no grammar restriction between sentences and between paragraphs. The co-occurrence is the basic link between representation components (e.g., connected sentences or connected paragraphs) occurring within the same larger components (e.g., paragraphs or sections). The coherence link between two co-occurred language components is an internal condition of understanding. The coherence link reflects the relevance, confirmation, explanation or derivation between representations. The external condition of understanding a representation component is that the directly cited components are understandable by readers. It is clear that a reader cannot understand a text if he/she does not understand most of its words. This indicates a semantic locality of representation and understanding [141].

The Locality of Interactive Semantics: *The semantics of a representation is rendered by a semantic image indicated by the components of the representation and the semantic links between the components. If the components have semantic links to other representations, only the direct semantic links contribute to the indication of the semantic image. The semantic image changes with interactions on the representation. The interactions through social network render a semantic locality.*

The indirect links pass their influence through the direct link if no direct link can be derived. The locality of interactive semantics has the following lemmas:

Lemmas of the locality of interactive semantics:

1. *Writing, reading and understanding are the processes of representation within the scope of current attention. The scope of attention can be a language component such as word, sentence and paragraph.*
2. *The components of a representation have more direct semantic links to each other than to the components of the other representations.*
3. *Understanding tends to arrange the representations semantically linked to one another within one region of understanding.* Understanding reaches wider region from local attention regions through semantic links.

An example is that the more common components (e.g., sentences) between two representations (e.g., paragraphs), the higher the possibility that they can be selected for understanding together, so they should be organized within one region. The extreme case is the repeat sentence. This locality is also a guidance of representation, including writing and organizing summaries.

The semantic locality is in line with the locality of computing as the reading and writing of the Turing machine is local to the tape.

Multi-Dimensional Locality: Locality is specific to dimension if representations are specified in a multi-dimensional space.

The purpose of representation is to indicate or derive meaning, which requests differences between representations. So, understandability and derivability are two folds of representation, which should be coordinated according to the estimated cognitive level of readers.

The additivity principle enables local representations to be composed to a larger representation or the global representation. The additivity principle and locality principle unveil an important phase of representation and understanding: *from local to global*.

After finishing a representation, understanding generates a representation in mind through reorganizing representations, *from global to local*: reorganizing relevant representations (e.g., sentences) within the global region into one region of a new representation.

The Locality of Understanding: Understanding is an unconventional mapping from an external representation like text into an internal mental representation (semantic image). Components appearing at different places can be mapped into one component of the new representation. The way of mapping is specific to individuals, which indicates the independence of understanding.

Locality and modularity have been studied in many disciplines such as philosophy, linguistics, software engineering and social network [39,42,89]. The locality of interactive semantics emphasizes three aspects: (1) Human understanding of a representation involves two processes: from local (e.g., a sentence) to global (e.g., the whole paper), and from global (e.g., the semantic image of the whole paper) to local (e.g., a concept); (2) The locality of interaction is the basis of generating and evolving semantics; and (3) Locality specific to dimension. The locality is a principle of summarization.

The following lemmas can be derived from the knowledge selection principle:

Suitable Summarizer:

1. *Authors who commonly cited a representation are the candidates of the suitable summarizers.* This is because the represented knowledge was shared and the knowledge for representation is at the same cognitive level with high probability.
2. *Authors are the best persons to summarize their own representations.* This is because authors have the knowledge for representation and the knowledge to be represented. However, authors have limited working time and may be influenced by individual characteristics (e.g., health, mood, and worldview) and social characteristics (e.g., culture, economy and influence).

As knowledge varies and evolves, the understanding of representation changes. Therefore it is not appropriate to use static criteria to evaluate summarization.

Relativity Principle: *Satisfactory summary is relative. A summary that satisfies one person may not satisfy the other.*

Different persons can make different summaries for the same text, and one person can generate different summaries for the same text at different stages of individual development. This is because knowledge of individuals evolves independently in mind while keeping a certain degree of communication. The relativity principle indicates the following principles:

Moderate Principle: *A summary can be only moderately satisfied.*

The moderate principle indicates that the best summary does not exist. So, the pursuit of the best summary is insignificant.

Dynamicity Principle: *The satisfied summaries of a representation vary with time.*

This is because knowledge, interest and understanding are specific to an individual and change with the evolution of knowledge and society.

Openness Principle: *A satisfied summary can be reached only through an open social process of interactions and representations.*

The openness principle implies that establishing static criteria for evaluating summarization is unnecessary, and that a closed system is incapable of reaching a satisfied summary.

The above fundamental characteristics and principles indicate the following strategies for summarization in an open environment consisting of humans, representations (e.g., texts), application systems, and summarizers.

Summarization strategies:

1. *Making use of the summaries of the summarizers who have rich links to the authors of the original text. More types of links render more common knowledge and experience* [138]. This is because the establishment of rich links indicates common individual characteristics and social characteristics.
2. *Adapting to readers' interests.* The interests of readers determine the selection of summaries. A good summarizer should know its potential readers. This requests a summarizer to collect and analyze readers' interests according to their reading behaviors and attitudes to summaries. This is to pursue a suitable summary rather than the best summary.
3. *Making summarization through human-machine interaction*, which can make full use of the advantages of both human and machines. It is the right way to pursue a satisfied summarization through a human-machine symbiotic system [62].

4. *Enabling different summaries to cooperate and compete with each other for impact at multiple dimensions* (e.g., acceptance for reading and adoption for generating new summaries). Ranking reviews to encourage contribution and competition among reviewers reflects social value in a summarization environment. Different summaries may represent different characteristics of the summarizer. Integrating individuals of diverse characteristics can encourage cooperation with each other in making new summaries.

5. *Transforming summarizations into the problem of searching suitable persons, summarizers or summaries within the semantic link networks consisting of authors, readers, summarizers, and representations.*

6. *Enabling summarizers to know the background of representations, including cultural, technological, social and economic concepts,* which help understand and compose representations. The key is to construct a semantic link network of concepts.

Implicit links in multi-dimensional space

7

Link and dimension are basic structures for understanding. The extent of recognizing the implicit links and the dimensions reflects the extent of understanding.

7.1 Implicit links

Implicit links exist between representations of different granularities. For texts, grammar provides the rules for connecting words. Implicit links connect sentences, enabling coherence between sentences and between paragraphs, to represent more complex meaning and enable readers to understand more complex representations.

Figure 7.1 depicts some implicit links within a paragraph selected from the Soul Mountain (the representative novel of Xingjian Gao, the first Chinese winner of the Nobel Prize in Literature). He renders a cute image of a lady by describing the features of her kerchief and the style of fastening the kerchief. The purpose of using Chinese here is to provide a case for English readers to check whether they can emerge the same image in mind according to the English words.

The author laid rich semantic links in this short text, which involves two hierarchies of category, representing two dimensions: *human* and *thing*. A *wear* link between the *lady* subcategory in the *human* category, and the *kerchief* subcategory in the *thing* category determines a group of ladies who wear the same style of kerchief. The word *kerchief* and the operation word "fasten" link the sentences on kerchief to render the category of kerchief. But there is no common word to connect the sentences on *lady*, and those sentences are placed in the front and the end rather than in neighbor. The concept of human body connects the sentences on the lady, face, features of face, chin, and the shape of body.

While reading, a reader maps the words in the text into the concepts in mind, which are further linked to the images in mind. The links are established through experience in cyberspace, physical space and social space. The mapping may not be one-to-one. Different people may make different mappings. A reader is likely to emerge the image of the lady through the following two categories: (1) kerchief, features of kerchief, and wearing style; and, (2) the features of face, and the shape of body. A reader without Chinese culture may not be able to emerge the same image as Chinese because of the difference of the links between words and concepts in minds.

To enable computers to better understand the text, human-level cyber-concepts need to be built in. The human-level cyber-concept not only includes the category hierarchy but also a concept mechanism that can simulate the mental concept.

Multi-Dimensional Summarization in Cyber-Physical Society. DOI: http://dx.doi.org/10.1016/B978-0-12-803455-2.00007-X

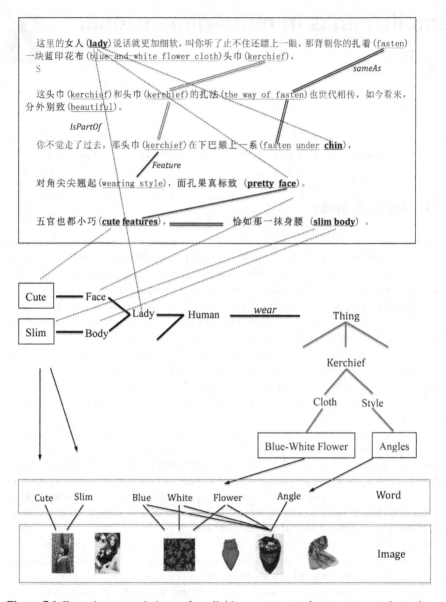

Figure 7.1 Emerging semantic image from linking sentences as larger representation units.

This example also explains the multi-dimensional locality because representations distributed in different places in text like the sentence on "lady" and the sentences on face, chin, and body are close in the category hierarchy.

The process of writing and reading accompany a process of weaving a semantic link network of language components in the text space. Figure 7.2 describes a network of writing a section of a scientific paper. "B D G" denotes the title of the section, which includes three language components (paragraph or sentence). A language

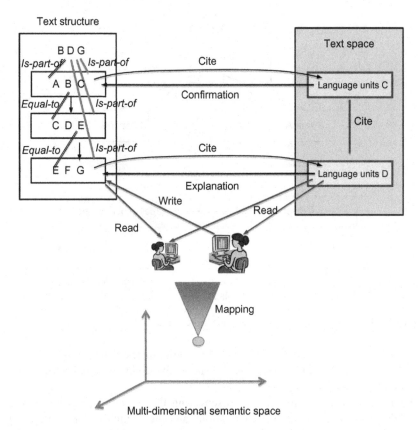

Figure 7.2 Mapping language representations into the semantic space through linking language units.

component can be a semantic link network of language representation components. The semantic link network includes such links as *equal-to*, *sequential* and *is-part-of*. The language components (*A, B, C*), (*C, D, E*), and (*E, F, G*) are understandable and derivable representations because different components (*A, B, D, F, G*) are connected and understood by sharing components (*C* and *E*).

The section is understandable because of the understandability principle. Connection can also be made by two different words that indicate the same thing. The writer uses the knowledge of language and the knowledge to be represented in his/her personal mental space while writing sentence by sentence. The reader emerges a semantic image in the personal semantic space while reading a sentence, and links different semantic images by linking sentences.

7.2   Discovering implicit semantic links

Some implicit semantic links can be established through reasoning on local links according to semantic link rules [141]. But the discovery of some implicit semantic

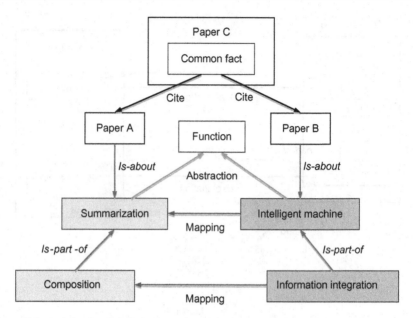

Figure 7.3 Deriving implicit links through analogical reasoning.

links needs reasoning on the semantic links between texts, including the citation link. Citations about common themes indicate similar links. Generalization provides the guidance of discovering implicit links.

Figure 7.3 shows an instance of discovering the semantic links between two methods. Paper A is about "summarization" and the "composition" is its component that composes the selected representation components into a summary. Paper B is about "intelligent machine" and the "information integration" is its component that integrates information of various types to support intelligent machines. If paper C cites paper A and paper B about a common theme, a similar link can be established between paper A and paper B. The condition that both "summarization" and "intelligent machine" can be abstracted as a function increases the similarity. The *is-part-of* link and the new similar link indicate the similar link between "composition" and "information integration." The derived semantic link indicates that the method of information integration for intelligent machine is probably useful for developing or improving the method of composition for summarization.

7.3   Observing from the psychological dimension

How humans remember and recall relations while reading text was regarded as the key to understanding text by many psychologists. Some psychologists regard text reading as a problem-solving process through discovering a set of cause-effect relations; some regard text reading as a process of linking the current sentence to previous understandings in memory.

With the problem-solving assumption, a text's causal structure was regarded as the primary determinant of recall. This structure is derived by parsing a text into individual states, then using the criterion "necessity in the circumstances" [116] to determine the causal links between those states. Therefore, "A is said to cause B if it is the case that B would not have occurred in the circumstances described by the text had A not occurred."

The causal structure of a text is an important determinant of how it will be understood and remembered. First, the more causal connections a state has to the rest of the text (either forward or backward), the better it will be recalled [45]. Second, a causal chain connecting a text's opening to its final outcome is recalled [115a] better than the states not on such a chain.

Some psychologists argue that the most likely causal antecedent to the next sentence is always held in short-term memory. This allows a reader to discover the causal structure of a text within the constraints of a limited-capacity short-term memory [36].

As a semantic link network of concepts [140], the semantic image is constructed and updated through reading and carrying out various reasoning during construction and after construction in the long-term memory.

7.4   Observing from the art dimension

One of the concerns of historical art study is the identification of the accurate times of artworks. For example, it was known that Vincent van Gogh's Rising Moon was painted in 1889 at Saint-Rémy-de-Provence in France, but nobody knows the exact time when it was done. To answer this question, a team traveled to the same location and identified the landmarks in the painting, which include an overhanging cliff that obscures a wedge of the luminous orange moon, and a distant double-roofed house. The team worked out the location where van Gogh was standing when he painted the canvas. The team measured the compass direction along which the moon appeared to him, and the height of the cliff above the horizon. Using the lunar tables and astronomy software, they then calculated the time and dates at which a rising full moon would appear above the horizon at that spot: May 16 and July 13, 1889. As the wheat in the painting is golden and harvested, it should be a date in July. Then they determined that it was painted on July 13, 1889 at 9:08 P.M. according to the report in *Nature* published June 13, 2003 (doi:10.1038/news030609-13).

This work can be interpreted by a mapping from the painting space into the physical space as shown in Figure 7.4. The painting space includes three dimensions: *time* (time of painting), *author*, and *type* (the type of the content such as landscape and people). The physical space includes two dimensions: *time* and *location*. The similar relation can be established between the painting and the real scene with the physical attributes: time and location, and lunar season help determine the

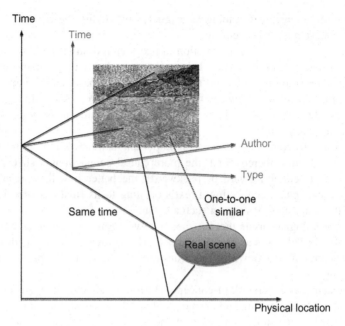

Figure 7.4 Discovering the physical attributes of the evening landscape with rising moon, 1889 by Vincent van Gogh.

missing attributes of the painting. The method can be extended to identifying the relation between a painting and a natural scene, and determining the relation between paintings can be identified in this space if their physical attributes are known.

General citation

8

Citation is widely used in scientific papers. In a general sense, citation is a special semantic link between two representations. Exploring citation is a way to explore the nature of summarization.

8.1   A dual semantic link network

A Semantic Link Network can be formally represented as: $SLN = <f\!\!: \{N, L\} \to T, O>$, where N is a set of semantic nodes, L is a set of semantic links, f is a mapping from $\{N, L\}$ into a common semantic space T such that every node in N and every link in L has a corresponding concept in T. T consists of a category hierarchy H and a rule set R for reasoning on semantic links. O is a set of operations that adds a node or a link to N or L, deletes a node or a link from N or L, *or maintains T*.

The maintenance operations on T include *add, update* or *remove* categories and rules for maintaining the structure of the category hierarchy.

Constant operations and reasoning evolve the semantic link network to render semantics. The evolution propagates the influence of operations from local range to wide range, then to the global network. The strategy of representation is from local to global: the semantic link connects local representations and influences wider representations through reasoning or various flows (e.g., knowledge flow through scientific publications).

From the computing point of view, *a semantic link network can be regarded as a complex computing process or a complex method*, where every semantic node represents one computing process (or method) and every semantic link represents the relation or data flow between computing processes or methods. According to this view, representation, method and computing are unified. Therefore, representation, method and computing can be studied uniformly. Summarizing texts can be extended to summarizing method and computing.

Reading and writing generate a semantic link network of language components (words or sentences) and a semantic link network of concepts described as follows:

$$<f\!\!:\{N,L\} \to T, O> - H - <f'\!\!:\{N',L'\} \to T', O'>,$$

where $<f\!\!: \{N, L\} \to T, O>$ represents the external semantic link network (e.g., the semantic link network of sentences within text), $<f'\!\!: \{N', L'\} \to T', O'>$ represents the internal (mental) semantic link network (e.g., semantic link network of concepts), H denotes humans or a system that operates the two semantic link networks and transforms between the external semantic link network and the

Multi-Dimensional Summarization in Cyber-Physical Society. DOI: http://dx.doi.org/10.1016/B978-0-12-803455-2.00008-1

internal semantic link network. *H* can interact with other individuals to build common semantic space and evolve individual semantic link networks.

This indicates the following principle of summarization.

Understandability of Summary: The summary of a representation (e.g., text) is understandable for a reader if the semantic link network of concepts within the summary can be mapped into the cognitive level of the reader and the reader's semantic link network of concepts on the original representation.

The semantic link network of concepts on the original representation is an important part of experience and knowledge for understanding the summary. Summarization following this principle means that the reader can use experience and basic knowledge to explain the representation. The problem is how to construct the internal semantic link network of concepts. A concept reflects the recognition of a physical object, an event or the abstraction of some objects or events. It can be regarded as a kind of computing, which inputs data of various types (e.g., a sentence or data obtained from sensors) and generates a model of the data. A solution to building concepts in cyberspace is to regard concepts as classes (like the classes in object-oriented programming or services in service computing), which can input a symbol representation and output an explanation of the input according to its rules and facts that can be collected from Wikipedia.

The symbol-concept dual semantic link networks indicate the following way to realize abstractive summarization:

(1) Discover the semantic link network of sentences in the original representation.
(2) Map the semantic link network of sentences into the semantic link network of concepts.
(3) Discover the hierarchy of semantic communities in the semantic link network of concepts.
(4) Select the appropriate abstraction level for the expected summary.
(5) Compose the summary by translating the abstract concepts into the symbol representation with the knowledge of language use.

The semantic net (or semantic network) and the correlational net were initially used for knowledge representation in AI and natural language processing [16,97,112]. The study of semantic net mainly focuses on three relations: *is-a* relation (one node is a kind of the other node), *implication* relation (one node implies the other node) and *action* relation (one node acts on the other node). Nodes are symbols indicating concepts.

The Semantic Web aims at a linked data platform on the Internet based on Web standards such as RDF (Resource Description Framework, https://www.w3.org/RDF/) and OWL (Web Ontology Language, http://www.w3.org/standards/semantic-web/). It tries to use triple representation, ontology and logic to define semantics.

Compared with the Semantic Web, the semantic link network is a study of the content networks. Its main task is to unveil the nature and the rules of evolving semantic link network where humans evolve in their lifetime, and to develop the method for discovering the semantic link network and making use of it. It uses a semantic space to specify the semantics of nodes and links, and conduct relational reasoning, which pursues rationality rather than correctness.

8.2 Citation

Citation is one of the basic elements of a scientific paper. Citation not only enables writers to represent thinking with the background (relevant representations in other papers) and the evidence (comparison with relevant representations, proved theories, verified models, etc.) through the sequential link of representations, but also enables readers to understand the author's thinking through the representations and the links to the background, and to convince the representation with the evidence from the cited representations. A chain of citations forms a structure that indicates the knowledge flow of authors. The introduction section of a scientific paper usually summarizes relevant papers by citing other papers.

Citation is a kind of basic local representation. The structure of citations indicates the global development of a research direction or an area. Citation involves reading, representation, selection, language use, and language understanding behaviors. Summarization is requested at the advanced stage of language development when the complex structure of representation emerges. It is necessary to understand citation when studying summarization.

Explicit citations are the components of scientific papers and books. A citation component consists of *representation* and *citation link*. A citation link may appear after the representation or in the middle of representation and takes such form as "[reference number]" or "(author, year)." For example: "In the Resource Space Model [134], a dimension is a method of categorization." An explicit citation component can be extracted by selecting the sentences in the paragraph that contain the citation link according to the language units (e.g., title, keywords) of the references.

A citation network forms and evolves with the formation and the development of a research area, although it does not exactly represent the semantics of the area. A research area emerges and evolves when papers on some concepts are accumulated and cited continually through time. As shown in Figure 8.1, a new paper A (denoting the title, author, abstract, etc.) becomes an often-cited paper and then becomes a source paper when the area is gradually formed. Meanwhile, the core representation (a set of key sentences) of the source paper develops toward the core representation of the papers of a research direction, and then develops toward the core representation of the area.

A survey paper summarizes an area by citing the important papers in the citation network, and it is often cited as it helps other researchers to quickly know this area. During the development of a research area, different survey papers may appear at different development stages or on different facets [1], the later survey paper can benefit from the summaries of previous survey papers. Citation and summarization are often involved in a reciprocity process [90].

Different from static text, the citation network dynamically renders the source, the formation and evolution of a study, the backbone, the impact of researchers and institutions, potential knowledge flows through citation links [135], and the networks of cooperation between researchers and between institutions with the evolution of the area. Summaries of different scales can be obtained through zoom-in-and-zoom-out on the citation network. It is feasible to transform a

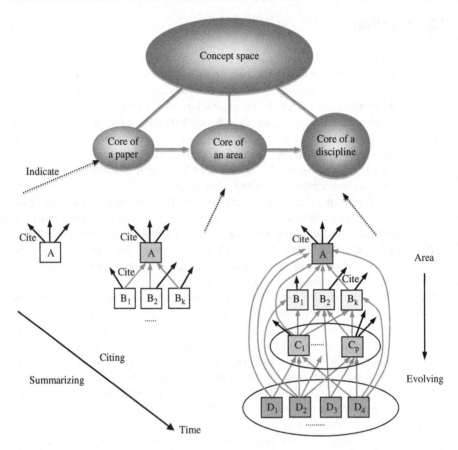

Figure 8.1 The thought of a researcher forms and develops with self-citing, citing other papers, and being cited by other papers. A research area emerges when new papers often cite some previous papers (the red arrows). The citation network evolves with partially summarizing an area and rendering research cores, important roles, relations and development tracks. The links between concepts indicated by the papers in the area are established and tightened with the evolution of the citation network. In microscopic, the implicit relations between language representation units of different granularities render the structures of papers and enrich the explicit citation structure.

citation network into a text by using some language patterns (for example, "the idea of A was extended by B," "the idea of A was used by B," and "the idea of A inspired B") to represent different citations, main roles, relations, and development track.

The citation networks in science provide richer indicators than isolated papers for analyzing a research area (including the roles of researchers, institutes, countries and papers), estimating the development of the areas, making decisions on research direction selection, and assessing the impacts of research.

The hyperlink of the Web is a kind of explicit citation that freely complements, explains, or extends the content of the current Web pages. Homepages like Yahoo are the summarizations of currently important Web pages. Different from scientific papers, webpages can be changed, and links can also be changed, so the hyperlink network of webpages evolves notably. An advanced faceted navigator provides a multi-facet summarization of the contents within a website for users to browse [129].

8.3 General citation

Implicit citation is often used in free texts and literature works. Some implicit citations have mark words such as *someone says, someone pointed out that ...*, and *according to someone's opinion*. These implicit citations can be located and transformed into explicit citation by searching these mark words and the references according to author names mentioned in text, and then inserting uniform citation marks as those in scientific papers. Some implicit citations just reuse others' sentences or clauses without any mark word. For example, the sentence "It's Greek to me!" appearing in text implicitly cites the scenario used in 1599 in Shakespeare's play Julius Caesar, and "into thin air" cites the book written by Jon Krakauer published in 1997 and many other earlier works. Transforming implicit citations needs to compare common clauses in works published in different times.

Citation is a kind of representation by individual selection and language use. Summarizing various citations can reach a notion of general citation.

Definition of General Citation: *Citation is an individual selection of representations for interpreting, evidencing, complementing, commenting, or revising a representation, either explicitly or implicitly, according to individual motivation and knowledge. Diverse individual selections evolve the citation network.*

8.4 Extension and intension

The notion of general citations forms the extension of representation and the intension of representation.

The extension of a representation A consists of the representations that cite A and the representations that are cited by A. If representation A cites a set of representations B, then B constitutes an extension of A. If representation A cites a set of representations B, and A is cited by a set of representations C, then both B and C constitute the extension of A.

The citation in the above definition includes implicit citation. The extension will expand with new citations. The characteristics of language use and understanding and the notion of general citation imply the following lemma:

Lemma: *If one person or system P cannot understand the extension of a representation A, P is not able to understand A, and if P understands the extension of a representation A P has the ability to understand A.*

The following are reasons:

(1) The extension actually represents all background knowledge of the representation.
(2) Authors use existing knowledge (knowledge for representation, knowledge to be understood, and common sense) to represent thinking because the purpose of writing is to enable the expected readers to understand.
(3) Readers use the existing knowledge to understand authors' thinking.
(4) Authors and readers have the same purpose: share knowledge and understand each other. The authors want more readers to understand their writings, and readers want to understand more about what they are reading.

The core representation renders the motivation and main idea of a representation. A good article renders one core. The core representation of a scientific paper is rendered by the cause-effect relations and the representations of some abstractive components that render the motivation and main idea, including title, keywords, abstract, introduction and conclusion. The representation that has a direct link to the core representation is a *close-core representation*. For example, two close language representations sharing some words are linked by these words. Representations linked to the close-core representations are relevant-to-core representation. Other representations are peripheral representations.

The intension of a representation is a concept or a semantic link network of concepts indicated by the intensions of the components of the representation and their relations.

The intension of a text is determined by the intensions of its paragraphs, the intension of a paragraph is determined by the intensions of its sentences, the intension of a sentence is determined by the intensions of words, and the intension of a word is determined by a basic concept.

The intension of a representation can be extended to include the citations from other representations. The intension of representation p is indicated by (1) *the core of p, Core(p)*, which may consist of the core representations of p; and, (2) *the representations that cite p.*

To facilitate understanding, the *intension* of a representation should be rendered by the common sense of a community. Some scientists tried to codify common sense to build computing systems to realize artificial intelligence [61]. Wikipedia shifted the paradigm of codifying common sense from personal effort to massive contribution with evolving a network of categories.

A core representation is often cited and used by other representations, and therefore it has wide extension. It is usually emphasized in various ways to attract attention. For scientific papers, a core representation reflects motivation, problem or solution, so it often appears in abstracts, introductions, the captions of figures, and conclusions. A paper may have several core representations but it helps understanding if a paper has just one core representation.

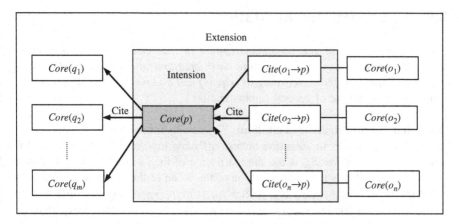

Figure 8.2 Extension and intension rendered by citation.

A core representation takes the priority of emerging while reading. The core representations usually appear in the front and in the end (e.g., title, abstract and conclusion) so that readers' short-term memory can be impressed before and after reading the main body. This helps enhance the memory of the core by focusing and refocusing on the core when building or retrieving the semantic images in the mental space.

Humans have been composing complex representations and making summarization through time, so we have the following axiom.

Axiom (Additive Axiom): *An understandable representation is a basic representation or it can be composed by a set of representations.*

This axiom is the basis of representation (in using and understanding languages) and summarization (especially, for multi-document summarization). Therefore, a representation p can be formalized as a structure of representations: $p = p$ (p) $| p \cup \ldots \cup p | \{p, \ldots, p\}$, which represents a recursive structure of an abstraction p (p), a union $p \cup \ldots \cup p$, and a set of representations $\{p, \ldots, p\}$.

This axiom is the consequence of composing through citing.

Figure 8.2 depicts the extension and the intension rendered by citations. Cite representation in scientific papers is rendered by the sentence or the paragraph that includes the cite mark commonly used within a community.

Dictionaries explain words in texts, so they can be regarded as the basic implicit citations to all texts. From this point of view, any text has a set of basic citations. So, the above statement is suitable for text.

For scientific papers, the intension of a paper p is its core rendered by the cause-effect relations and the abstractive representation, and the union of the core and the representations in other papers that cite p. The extension of a paper p is the union of the intensions of all papers that are cited by p and the intensions of all papers that cite p.

8.5   Summarization as citation

The basic behaviors of general summarization include emerging, selecting, citing (explicitly or implicitly), and organizing representations at language level, concept level and knowledge level according to requirement and motivation. Text summarization is a special case of general summarization.

Definition (Summarization as citation): *The summarization S of a set of representations P is defined by its intension Intension(P) and extension Extension(P) as follows*, where $S(Intension(P))$ is the summarization of the intension of P, $S(Intension(P) \cup Extension(P))$ is the summarization of the union of the intension of P and the extension of P, $p \rightarrow p'$ means that p cites p', $\{Cite(p_i \rightarrow p) \mid i \in [1, \ldots, m]\}$ denotes the set of cite representations in p_i that cites p, and $Cite(p_i \rightarrow p)$ describes p from the view of the author of p_i. The union refers to set union or graph union if the intension and extension take the form of sets or graphs.

$S(P) = <S(Intension(P)), S(Intension(P) \cup Extension(P))>$.

$Intension(P) = \{ <Intension(p), \ldots, Intension(p)> \mid p \in P\}$.

$Intension(p) = \{ <Core(p), Core(p) \cup Cite(o_k \rightarrow p) \mid k \in [1, \ldots, n], p \in P, o_k \in P>$.

$Extension(P) = \{ \cup Extension(p) \mid p \in P\}$.

$Extension(p) = \{Intension(q_i) \cup Intension(o_j) \mid p \rightarrow q_i, o_j \rightarrow p, i, j \in [1, \ldots, n]$, $p \in P$, $q_i \in P, o_j \in P\}$.

Different from the previous notions of summarization, this definition gives the minimum summary (the summary of the intension) and the maximum summary (the summary of the intension and the extension) of a representation, and it regards citation as the fundamental behavior and mechanism of summarization.

Citation is a basic operation of representation. Accompany indicating, interpreting, extending, and structuring representations, citation network evolves to render the formation and evolution of concepts and knowledge flows. From this point of view summarization is a process of creating a citation to the source.

Dimensions of summary

9

The fundamental scientific problem of realizing an intelligent summarization is the think lens based on multi-dimensional semantic computing. Dimension can be regarded as a method of categorization, which enables computing to zoom along multiple dimensions on the representations of different levels according to the rules of different dimensions. The computing model will be greatly changed if dimensions themselves are regarded as computing.

9.1 Dimension as computing

Generally, a dimension uniquely specifies a point in a space with the least number of independent coordinates, and a dimension usually takes the form of a vector of variants like the Vector Space Model [104, 105].

The Resource Space Model is a multi-dimensional category space, where every dimension is a category hierarchy [134]. From the computing point of view, a dimension is a category of computing methods on a set of representations D: $X = \{C_1, \ldots, C_n\}$, where $C_1, \ldots$, and C_n are the computing components of X such that the computing result forms a partition or category hierarchies on D. The computing can be carried out by either humans or computer: inputting representations and then outputting category hierarchies.

Different dimensions $X_1, \ldots$, and X_n on the same representation set D constitute a multi-dimensional method space $(X_1, \ldots, X_n)$ such that every point in the space is the common output of every dimension.

The systematic theory of the multi-dimensional category space, including query capability and expressive power of the multi-dimensional category space and the relations between search efficiency and the number of coordinates, was unveiled as a part of the Resource Space Model [134].

Dimension as computing extends the notion of dimension as variant. The relational data model reflects a view of attributes. The object-oriented model reflects a view of abstraction on objects. The Multi-Dimensional Resource Space Model reflects a view of abstraction on contents, methods and computing.

9.2 The dimensions for structuring summary

Structuring summary in an appropriate form is important, as summary is mainly for humans to read and understand. An appropriate form concerns an innovative cyber

Multi-Dimensional Summarization in Cyber-Physical Society. DOI: http://dx.doi.org/10.1016/B978-0-12-803455-2.00009-3

display based on human mental structure, psychological structure and innovative display. The following are some high-level dimensions for organizing a summary.

(1) **Time**. *Organizing representations in the order of time, e.g., the time of the events described in the representation or the time of publishing the papers that contain the representation.* The time order is in line with the human innate sense of time and the process of reading. The time order reflects the flow of thought when representations are formed and understood.

(2) **Knowledge flow**. The knowledge of the writer is fused with the knowledge of the readers, who represent their knowledge in their writings. In scientific publication, the flow of thought is formed through citation. A flow may be separated into some branches along with the expansion of the citation network.

(3) **Category of contents**. Contents form with evolving categories when authors write and cite explicitly or implicitly. This is relevant to (2) because the separation of categories forms branches in citation network. Contents can be classified into different categories when explicit citations are not available or unknown, and the categorization of the contents provides another way to investigate the knowledge flow.

(4) **Author**. *The original structure of the core representations takes the priority to appear in summary.* The reason is that authors are the best persons to organize their representations. Experienced authors can have their own patterns in organizing representations.

(5) **Reader**. The reader's interest takes the priority to appear if reader has a particular request. The reason is that summarization is to provide service for readers.

(6) **Core**. A core representation, rendered by the features such as location, font size and color, indicates the author's emphasis, which facilitates understanding. *Relevant representations are arranged at the places close to the core representation.* This priority arranges relevant representations distributed in the original representation at the places close to the core representations in the summary. This is a kind of semantic locality [139]. One representation or a set of representations can have multiple cores that render dimensions (or facets [129]).

(7) **Formation Order**. For a set of closely relevant representations, the order of organizing representations in a summary should consider *the formation process* of the set, which reflects certain semantics of the set. Citation between scientific papers reflect such an order, which should be considered in multi-document summarization. The linear order of traditional text representations is in line with human physiological characteristics and innate sense of order. It is unclear so far how the human mind organizes knowledge. Combining the linear organization with the order of generalization and specialization can reflect not only reading characteristics but also understanding characteristics.

Organizing representations in a multi-dimensional space enables readers to know the representations from different dimensions. For example, a reader can know not only the interested summary but also the representation from the author's priority.

We can consider organizing representations in a multi-dimensional categorization space. A dimension like a topic can organize coordinates as a tree representing multi-level generalization and specialization. Sub-dimensions can be arranged according to the measure of relevance between coordinates. Figure 9.1 shows a three-dimensional space for organizing representations through time dimension, author dimension and topic dimension. It enables readers to know the topic movement of a particular author or a group of authors through time. It also enables readers to know the role of the author such as the source and the novice during the

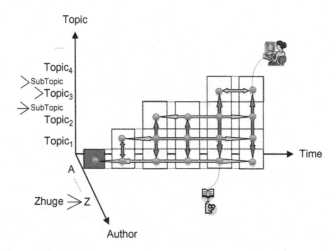

Figure 9.1 A three-dimensional space for organizing representations. The two-way arrows represent possible browse threads through the dimensions of time, topic and author.

development of a topic at a certain time. The multi-dimensional organization can provide multiple threads for readers to browse as indicated by the two-way arrows:

(1) Generalization thread and specialization thread through a topic tree.
(2) Time thread within a topic.
(3) Topic relevancy thread within a period at the time dimension.
(4) The evolution of topics in the area through the time dimension.

Humans experience in a multi-dimensional space but have to use a two-dimensional media such as paper and screen to externalize representation. Information is lost through the transformation from the internal representation to the form of display. Inventing a new interface that can easily convey the representations through multiple channels will extend human understanding and the way to representation.

A multi-dimensional space can be represented in different forms [134]. Figure 9.2 shows a space with four dimensions: *topic, region, time* and *author*, each of which is regulated by a tree structure. Every point in the space has one projection at every dimension (a node in the tree). Moving from one point to another point changes the projections at every dimension of the space. This form of representation can represent a space of any number of dimensions. This form of representation looks similar to the wind-rose plot, which can efficiently convey the meaning of how wind speed and direction are typically distributed at a location. The difference is that the win-rose plot specifies the uniform value: speed, while a point in the multi-dimensional space can have different types of values (projections) at different dimensions.

Artists have made great efforts to summarize multi-dimensional impressions in minds on the two dimensional physical medias such as papers and canvas. Cubism is one stream of painting led by Pablo Picasso (Spanish, 1881–1973) and Georges Braque (French, 1882–1963). Figure 9.3 makes an intuitive comparison between the impression of Cubism and the impression of natural language. Understanding

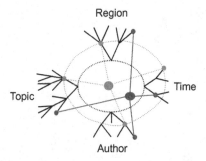

Figure 9.2 A form of displaying multi-dimensional space.

Figure 9.3 The impression of Cubism and the impression of natural language. Left: Girl with a Mandolin, 1910 by Pablo Picasso. Right: La Guitare, 1911−1912 by Georges Braque.

requires the mappings between external representations and internal representation (semantic image) in minds.

It is a challenge to intelligent systems to generate a new picture as a summary according to a piece of text.

It is not difficult to collate a picture from a set of existing pictures according to the understanding of the text if an existing semantic link network of pictures and language representation units can be established. The key issue is to lay out the pictures and to determine the criteria of assessment. It is difficult to collate a beautiful picture that matches human requirements and the criteria of beauty. It is a grand challenge to create a picture from the basic elements like pixels according to the understanding of a piece of text, because there is a big gap between the semantics of the basic elements and the semantics of the whole picture.

9.3 Summarization ondemand

Summarization is carried out in an interactive environment where people read, write, cite and communicate within personal spaces. The personal spaces reflect personal

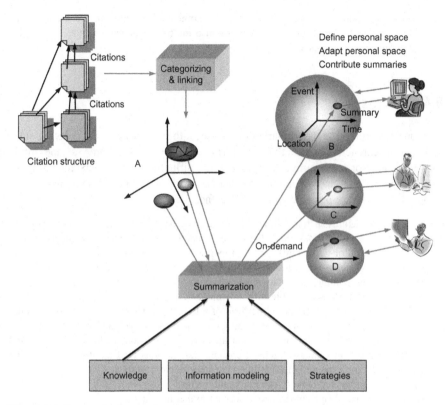

Figure 9.4 Summarization on demand.

reading experience, interests and knowledge based on the texts that have been read. A summarization can be satisfied only when it matches the personal space of the reader.

The general process of summarization ondemand is shown in Figure 9.4. The summarization system is responsible for categorizing, linking and reorganizing representations. The function "Categorizing & Linking" categorizes representations according to the given dimensions, connects representations by discovering implicit relations, transforming implicit relations into explicit relations, discovering communities, and identifying appropriate representations. Users can adapt the dimensions to generate new summaries and to add summaries to the system for composition, comparison, comment and adoption. Citation links between summaries and source representations help analysis and reuse. The information modeling provides the appropriate models for processing and organizing representations. The knowledge provides the rules for representation and understanding. The summarization strategies support the processing of representations under uncertain conditions.

The arrows in red denote the following transformations:

(1) Transform representations (including, citation structure) into a multi-dimensional category space (denoted as *A* in the figure) by categorizing and linking representations.

(2) Transform a point or a subspace of *A* into a point or a subspace in the user personal spaces (denoted as *B*, *C* and *D*), which are also multi-dimensional category spaces that represent users' interests and personalities.

9.4 Forms

Previous research on text summarization neglects the innovation of displaying summary as researchers assume that the form of output is the same as the input. However, the form of summary significantly influences the understandability of summary. Interface innovation enables users to easily understand a summary.

The following are possible forms of interface:

(1) *Structure.* Structures such as list, table, tree and grid have been widely used by people to summarize representations in daily life, e.g., displaying the table of contents, family trees, organization structures, and properties on maps. Different structures are suitable for different applications. The appropriate combination of these structures can represent more complex text than single structure. For particular applications like sport news, a simple table is a suitable form of summary.

(2) *Hypertext.* A summary can be in the form of a hypertext, where some texts are summarized as a hyperlink, and some texts containing hyperlinks are summarized as a hyperlink at the higher level. The advantage is that the content is the same as the original text and readers can read the concise top-level content first and then read the details by clicking the link they are interested in. The following steps implement this:
 (a) Give the expected scale of summary and interest.
 (b) Rank the paragraphs of the text according to the interest.
 (c) Shrink the low rank paragraphs as hyperlinks.
 (d) Do (a) if the scale of the text is larger than expected, otherwise end. Automatic link generation was studied in hypertext area [105]. An interactive visual text analysis tool can help readers understand the summary [65].

(3) *Semantic linking network.* A semantic linking network can clearly summarize the main concepts and cues within text(s) [138,140]. A semantic link network of important concepts and relations can help readers quickly know the main cues and measures in representations. The key is how to extract appropriate nodes and links from representations. Different from the linear reading, a semantic link network enables readers to know a general view and the main measures of large representations immediately. The semantic link network can be regarded as the map of the cyberspace and social space.

(4) *Multimedia.* Coordinating texts, pictures and videos can render a summary from different channels of sense. It is particularly useful in making slides or posters for scientific research according to papers and in summarizing historical and literature works. A semantic link network is a way to meaningfully organize multimedia.

(5) *Emerging.* This function is to emerge pictures or video clips relevant to the important representations within viewing scope while displaying. An eye tracking mechanism can help automatically locate the scope. Evaluation is needed to ensure the effectiveness of reading.

(6) *New devices.* New interface devices like the 3D monitor will significantly influence the representation of summary. Optimizing the layout of display needs to consider three

dimensions. A 3D printer extends the display from cyberspace to the physical space. A 4D printer will further extend display to the formation of the objects sensed from more dimensions. The advanced summarizer could create new objects that can be seen, touched, smelled, heard and even tasted. People could hold what they think and write. The new interfaces provide a new cognitive environment for human development.

There are two dimensions of criteria for selecting the form: (1) accuracy in conveying the core of the original representation, and (2) reader familarity.

Multi-dimensional evaluation

10

Evaluation is a systematic determination of the merit, value and significance of a method by using objective criteria or comparison with existing methods. It is widely used in the cases where formal methods are not applicable.

Previous evaluation methods for summarization focus on result (summary) and human experience, which mainly fall into two categories: (1) *Criteria-based*, setting up criteria or public data set as the standards for evaluation. Criteria can be on the internal structure (e.g., coherence and coverage) of the summary or on the impact on tasks including relevance and understandability. Public data set is for comparing summaries generated by different summarization methods. (2) *Human-based*, inviting people to read the summary and then give scores or compare the summary with the summaries written by people. The first method seems objective but it still relies on the people who make the criteria.

It is hard to build a fair gold-standard for evaluating all summaries. The characteristics of language use and understanding determine that it is insignificant to pursue the best summary. It is an undecidable problem to evaluate a summary, as evaluation is not about correct or incorrect.

Summarization is involved in individual construction process and social construction process, which carries out along multiple dimensions. The basic characteristics and principles of language use and understanding indicate the following dimensions of evaluation:

(1) **Reader**. It consists of the following sub-dimensions:
   (a) *Interest*. A summary should match the interests of readers. Sometimes, readers only need one dimension of a representation. Readers' comments and previous reading behaviors (e.g., the frequently clicked hyperlinks) reflect interests.
   (b) *Cognitive level*. A summary should match the reader's cognitive level. Therefore, concepts within the scope of the reader's cognitive level should be selected in summary.
   (c) *Reader cognitive space*. A multi-dimensional category space can be built to simulate the reader's cognitive space. Summarization should consider the current interest points and the cognitive level in the cognitive space.
(2) **Author**. A summarizer can understand the input representation better if the summarizer knows more about the author, including the relevant articles and the social networks of authors and readers. A cognitive space of authors can also be established to represent authors' understandings.
(3) **Input**. Input should also be evaluated because not all representations are necessary for summarization. On one hand, a very simple and short representation such as one sentence of a short message, a short paragraph of text and a picture is unnecessary for summariza-

Multi-Dimensional Summarization in Cyber-Physical Society. DOI: http://dx.doi.org/10.1016/B978-0-12-803455-2.00010-X

tion because they can be understood at a glimpse. On the other hand, the input should be within readers' interest scope.

(4) Summarizer.

  (a) *Openness*. The closed systems designed by particular persons are unable to make a satisfied summarization because only the persons sharing knowledge with the writer can make a summary that keeps consistency with the source.

  (b) *Adaptability*. A summarization system should be improvable during use, and be able to adapt to readers' updates and adapt to new representations (especially on the same topic).

  (c) *Interactivity*. This also implies that a summarizer should be able to interact with readers so that it can select the appropriate representations (e.g., sentences) and use the representations that the reader is familiar with. Further, it should interact with other people (including authors) to get more concepts and rules, and with the other application systems to get more information.

(5) Output (Summary). It includes the following sub-dimensions:

  (a) *Core representation*. The core representations of the source and the relations between them should be reserved in summary for general-purpose summarization.

  (b) *Coherence*. Coherence between representations (e.g., sentences) can increase readability [10,13].

  (c) *Completeness*. A summary should be self-complete: all core representations that match a reader's interest should be included.

(6) Usage. It is about people (the number of people and their interests) who have used the summary and their attitudes on the summary.

(7) Question-Answer. Different representations can support human or agents who read to answer different questions. A set of questions Q and the corresponding answer set A can be determined for the input R first. If the answer A to Q can also be generated according to the representation r that contains fewer representation units than R, then r is a suitable summary for Q. This requests that r contains the same concepts as A and Q, and there is a link between the concepts about Q and the concepts about A. Question-answer evaluation narrows down the interest scope of readers and makes the evaluation more focused on questions.

Evaluation is a part of the study on summarization. It interprets and predicts the value and effect of a method. The multi-dimensional methodology suggests that input (source), summarization, output (summary) and evaluation should be evaluated in a multi-dimensional category space where people interact and understand each other. Evaluation itself evolves with the development of the study of summarization and other studies. Evaluation based on big data provides a more reliable interpretation and prediction for a new method.

Incorporating pictures into a summary

11

Pictures can give people a quicker and more intuitive impression than natural lan-guage representation. Pictures use a different language from the natural language to convey information. Incorporating pictures into texts provides an additional lan-guage dimension for writers to represent and for readers to understand the representation.

11.1 Advantages

On Facebook, photos perform best for likes, comments, and shares as compared to texts, videos, and links (http://danzarrella.com/infographic-how-to-get-more-likes-comments-and-shares-on-facebook.html).

It is significant to incorporate pictures into a summary because (1) pictures and texts play different roles in rendering meaning: it is hard to describe the meaning of some pictures in words, and it is also hard to represent the meaning of some texts with pictures; (2) pictures have become more and more important means to render meaning in daily life with the wide use of smart phones; and, (3) people have rich experience in understanding pictures, so incorporating pictures into a summary can increase the understandability of a summary. Many summarization applications have incorporated pictures, e.g., transforming a paper into slides or a poster, trans-forming a novel into a cartoon book, and creating a webpage according to a set of texts and pictures.

Figure 11.1 shows a webpage, which is an example of human summarization with pictures, texts and hyperlinks.

Figure 11.2 shows two summaries of news about China's submission of its first robotic moon rover. The left-hand side is the text-only summary and the right-hand side is the summary incorporating relevant pictures. There are different ways to arrange pictures in displays but pictures should be selected according to the core representation and arranged near the core sentences according to the semantic local-ity principle as discussed before [139]. This example arranges pictures beside the related text. The summary with pictures is more attractive than the text-only sum-mary. A picture can convey meaning in about 1−10 seconds due to its familiarity and complexity to the viewer. In contrast, readers need to scan the whole text to know the pure text summary.

Pictures take the priority in conveying meaning while reading the summary with pictures. There are different reading orders, for example: (1) browse all pictures first and then read the text beside each picture, and (2) view one picture first and then read

Multi-Dimensional Summarization in Cyber-Physical Society. DOI: http://dx.doi.org/10.1016/B978-0-12-803455-2.00011-1

Figure 11.1 Human summarization with pictures and hyperlinks.

China's Chang'e 3 moon lander and its Yutu rover touched down on the moon Saturday (Dec. 14) at about 8:11 a.m. EST (1311 GMT), though it was late Saturday night local time at the mission's control center in Beijing during the landing.	A Chinese rocket carrying the Jade Rabbit moon rover blasts off from the Xichang. The lander carries the moon rover called Yutu, or "Jade Rabbit" which was launched onboard the Chang'e 3 rocket on 1 December.
China's first robotic moon rover 140-kilogram (300-pound) "Jade Rabbit" rover separated from the much larger landing vehicle early Sunday, around seven hours after the unmanned Chang'e 3 space probe touched down on a flat, Earth-facing part of the moon leaving deep tracks on its loose soil, state media reported Sunday, several hours after the country successfully carried out the world's first soft landing of a space probe on the moon in nearly four decades.	The Chang'e 3, named after a lunar goddess, on Saturday managed the first "soft landing" on the moon since 1976, the official Xinhua news agency reported. In Chinese folklore, the shapes on the moon are a lady with a rabbit on the moon.
China's English language Xinhua reported on December 14, 2013 that the Yutu or Jade Rabbit rover has deployed from the Chang'e 3 lunar lander and has begun to roll across the lunar surface on the moon's Bay of Rainbows.	China has sent into space on December 2, Chang'e- 3's Moon exploration tool performs a soft landing on the moon was successful. 21:10 local time at (15:10 BST) successful soft landing on the moon with the realization of China in the world, after the United States and the Soviet Later, the six-wheeled rover will survey the moon's geological structure and surface and look for natural resources for three months, while the lander will carry out scientific explorations at the landing site for one year.
China has reported landing its Jade Rabbit rover on the moon, in the first soft landing of a rover in nearly four decades today, the latest step in the country's ambitious space programme.	
China's moon rover "Yutu" (Jade Rabbit) went to sleep	Jade Rabbit, or Yutu, will start sending back data and pictures from Sinus Iridum, or the Bay of Rainbows, a basaltic plain formed from lava that filled a crater. 'Jade Rabbit' Rover Basks in Lunar Bay of Rainbows.

Figure 11.2 A pure text summary and a summary incorporating pictures.

the beside text, ..., view the last picture and then read the text beside it. Pictures and texts may be viewed again but pictures still take priority during reviewing.

Further, the two types of summaries have different memory effects. The summary incorporating pictures can enhance reader's short-term and long-term memory. An explanation is that the summary with pictures gives readers stronger impressions and provides more dimensions for rendering meaning, and establishes more links to render meaning.

The structure of text with pictures request readers to use a quick reading method, which does not follow the sequential order of sentences as traditional texts. Chapter 16 will discuss quick reading in depth.

A picture taken by a camera is an image of the physical space while natural language representation indicates a semantic image in mind. A summary rendered by both pictures and natural language provides rich indicators for readers to build semantic images.

For extractive text summarization, maintaining consistency between sentences can enhance readability. One advantage of incorporating pictures into a summary is that pictures provide a different type of link between language units (e.g., sentences), especially when the connection sentence cannot be found in the original text. For example, the picture with tags *a* and *b* (e.g., *hotel* and *garden*, indicating "a picture of *hotel* with nice *garden*") can bridge the sentence containing *a* (e.g., *garden*, indicating "It is a beautiful *garden*") and the sentence containing *b* (e.g., *hotel*, indicating "The *hotel* is near the sea"). This new type of link can enhance the readability of a summary.

New generation search engines have integrated pictures and summaries into search results. The summaries of texts and hyperlinks in their formatted search results provide richer contents for users than the link list provided by the old search engines. However, a pre-designed format is limited in its ability to adapt to diverse user requirements.

11.2   Strategies

The following are some problems and strategies.

(1) *How to select appropriate pictures?* Humans are specialized in recognizing pictures as they experience and reflect the physical space and build semantic image in mind. However, machines need to rely on human instruction to process pictures. Web 2.0 enables people to upload and tag pictures on the Web. The *semantic link networks of texts, pictures, tags and users indicate a kind of social semantics of picture usage and thus provide the ground for selection*. So building the networks is the key to solving the problem. From the evolution construction and social construction point of views [141], tags might have been used in some texts by people. *Language representations like tags indicate the usage of the pictures.* Existing approaches such as feature-based approaches and machine learning approaches can be used to classify pictures. Image retrieval techniques can help find candidate pictures [48].

(2) *How to organize pictures and texts?*
  (a) Use pictures to replace the corresponding representations in the original text, to summarize the representation, and to organize the summary according to the original structure.
  (b) Select and use pictures to replace the texts in a summary.
  (c) Select and insert pictures into a summary at appropriate places.
  (d) Classifying pictures from multiple dimensions including time and location, which help distinguish pictures of different dimensions so that appropriate pictures can be selected to match the text in the summary.

(e) Construct a semantic link network of pictures, tags and language representations in relevant texts as the summary. A semantic link can be regarded as a general citation that semantically connects two things [140].

(3) *How to identify events in pictures and link them to appropriate texts?* *A strategy is to make use of sensors and create semantic links between pictures and texts by detecting common projections at the physical dimension and social dimension.* Current smart cameras (e.g., smart phones) can record the time and physical location of taking photos, which are the projections of pictures on the time dimension and the location dimension. The photos are probably relevant to the events happening at the same time and location that holds artefacts (e.g., building) and people.

Using pictures to summarize text is a new direction of summarizing text. Empirical research has been done in this direction [2,121,132]. Research can lead to a new form of summary that can increase readability and understandability. Online picture-sharing systems like Flicker provide rich picture resources for implementing this idea. As new pictures are continually added to the online systems, a good summarization system should be able to keep up-to-date pictures in summarization.

Figure 11.3 depicts the idea of constructing a semantic link network of pictures and tags as a summary. The core words such as "CIKM2012," "hotel," "golf" and "garden" can be identified by comparing the source text and tags. Then, the relations like "back of" relying on the core words can be identified. So, the techniques of text summary can be extended to the construction of semantic link network and image retrieval [48]. Further, pictures can be extended to the snapshots of videos. Different from image retrieval (e.g., search images according to keywords), the picture-based summarization approach has a groundwork of texts (a network of source texts or summaries) when searching the picture-text repository.

The generated summary is not unique as the tag sets of different pictures may be overlapped. Existing summaries can be put into the space and linked to the tag set. In this way, the existing summaries can be reused when making new summarizations.

It is important to ensure that the generated network of symbols and images should be small to facilitate understanding. According to the principle of efficiency and the principle of semantic locality, the radius of the network should be small. The radius can be defined as *the maximum length of link chain from the center (determined by the core nodes) to any node.* In real application, a summarization system should enable readers to adjust the radius according to requirement.

Incorporating pictures into a summary enables a summarizer to summarize events. Events can be classified into points in a complex space with the following dimensions:

(1) *Time.* Dimensions evolve with time. Different types of events may have different distributions at the time dimension.

(2) *Location.* An event happens at a physical location, which can be captured by devices such as GPS, IP, or communication network.

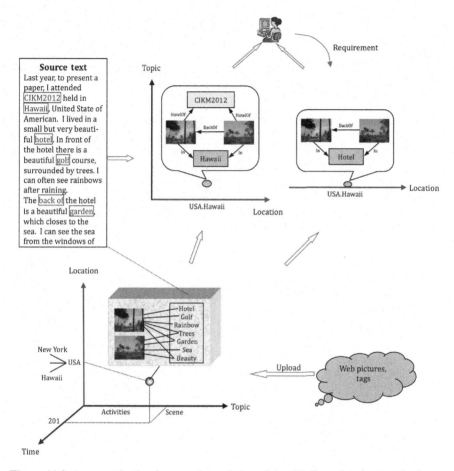

Figure 11.3 A summarization framework consisting of a multi-dimensional categorization space of summary in form of semantic link network of pictures and language representations and a requirement space defined and managed by users.

(3) *People*. Different classes of people play different roles in society and thus are likely involved in different events.

(4) *Category*. A hierarchy of categories.

(5) *Representation*. It usually includes some sub-dimensions: *feature representation*, *pattern representation*, *language representation* (including text, voice, and movie), and *function representation* (different objects such as car, mobile phone, house and road have different functions).

Different from pictures taken by cameras, paintings represent the artists' observations, thinking and emotions in a particular language of painting (e.g., Chinese ink painting).

Summarizing videos, graphs and pictures

12

The problem of summarizing texts, pictures, and videos can be generalized as one problem. The relations between texts, between pictures, and between videos can be mutually enforced, explained and rendered. The form of summary can be a semantic link network of texts, pictures, audios, and videos.

12.1 Summarizing videos

People are spending more and more time on videos. Online statistic data show that viewers are 85% more likely to purchase a product after watching a product video, 85% of the US Internet audiences watch videos online, over 60 hours of videos are uploaded each minute onto YouTube, and 700 YouTube videos are shared on Twitter every minute.

Automatic video summarization is to generate a clip of a long video or a set of long videos. It is important in video management, retrieval and browsing. It becomes more and more important with the wide use of digital cameras in our society for security, news, entertainment, education, advertisements, etc. Humans are able to make operations to summarize a movie according to their understandings and requirements, but are limited in ability to view and summarize huge volumes of videos generated every day. Automatic video summarization can help humans quickly know the core content in big video volumes.

There are two fundamental classes of video summarization: (1) focusing on still pictures (static storyboard), a small collection of salient images extracted from video sources; and, (2) focusing on moving pictures (moving storyboard), a collection of image sequences, and the corresponding audio abstract extracted from the original sequence, which results in a short video clip.

Summarizing a video requires machines to identify the essential characteristics of the video. Video summarization concerns the simplification of motion. A video sequence can be represented as trajectory curves in a high-dimensional feature space, which can be decomposed into curve segments of low dimension for simplification [28]. The patterns of events, conversations, and behaviors should be characterized to get semantically meaningful summaries of complicated video contents [117]. Low-level features such as color, boundary, and shot classification can help summarize videos. For particular applications like football games [32], important sections such as slow-motion segments and goals in games are known by humans, so it is easy to find the important sections. Some criteria such as *coverage* (the summary should represent the original one) and *diversity* (the elements of the summary

Multi-Dimensional Summarization in Cyber-Physical Society. DOI: http://dx.doi.org/10.1016/B978-0-12-803455-2.00012-3

should be distinct from each other) were proposed [111]. Some approaches focus on some contents about who, what, where, and when in the framework of the video contents to produce a concept-level summary [17]. Existing research is generally empirical and focuses on particular applications.

Modern movies provide more channels (e.g., voice and music) for understanding than early silent movies. Current online movies contain subtitles, which provide a new condition for making summarization of videos through natural language processing. These subtitles provide the basis for generating a piece of text as the summary of movies.

A semantics-based approach to summarizing videos is to construct a semantic structure on videos by introducing semantic links into videos. The higher abstraction level of the structure presents a more general summary of the video. A semantic link network of video components enables users to query the interested components and navigates in the network according to interest, e.g., the semantic link network of video components represents the main thread of a story development.

To realize more meaningful video summarization, it is important to represent body language, spoken language, emotion, habit and psychological activities in microscopic level. Behavior recognition is the basic components of understanding videos. In macroscopic level, it is important to represent the background of the video and relevant social structure, interests, fashion, rules, regulations, laws and culture of society in a summarization system. These concern in-depth understanding of the basic interaction principles in the complex space consisting of cyberspace, social space and physical space.

12.2   Summarizing graphs

Graphs are the generalization of various real networks in cyberspace (e.g., data structures), physical space (e.g., supply chains, material flow networks) and social space (e.g., social networks of things).

Summarizing data structures can provide more general data services. The summarization of a relational database takes a table as input and produces a reduced version of the table through rewriting and generalization. The resulting table is expected to provide tuples with less precision than the original but more informative [106]. Summarizing data streams supports more general fundamental queries on data streams such as point, range, and inner-product queries [24]. Fuzzy set was used to summarize data structures [99,130]. The Resource Space Model supports multi dimensional generalization and specialization [134,141]. Transformation between different data structures can help summarization [134]. A unified representation such as Extensible Markup Language (XML) and Web Ontology Language (OWL) helps transformation and unify summarization.

Summarization can help humans understand large-scale graphs. Summarizing a large-scale graph of data is important to graph data management as it can render the patterns hidden in data [87,119]. An interactive graph summarization approach was proposed [139]. Statistics is a useful means for machines to summarize graphs. Network analysis techniques such as degree distribution and community discovery can be used to find more important parts and the hierarchy of a graph.

In some areas like CAD, graph components have formal specifications. Making abstraction on graph components can be done through mathematical derivation. So, these areas have the requirements of summarization and the correctness guarantee of using summaries.

If we regard a text as a graph of words or sentences, text summarization can be regarded as a problem of summarizing a semantic link network [138], where nodes and edges can be texts, pictures and videos.

12.3 Summarizing pictures

The main purpose of summarizing pictures is to select a small set of pictures from a large set of pictures and make the necessary arrangement according to interest. There are more and more real requirements of summarizing pictures with the explosion of digital pictures online in recent years due to the wide deployment of cameras and popularity of smart phones. The summarization of pictures also helps incorporate appropriate pictures into the summary as discussed before.

Humans can make a humanized summarization because they have experience and knowledge beyond pictures. It is difficult to enable machines to make a humanized summarization. Discovering the semantic link networks in which the pictures are involved can help automatic summarization. Automatic summarization of pictures can be extended to include the solutions to the following issues:

(1) *Generating a piece of text to represent a set of pictures.* A solution is to transform this issue into an information retrieval and text summarization issue: Select the representative tags of these pictures, search relevant texts according to these tags (or select the texts that contain or link to these pictures), and then summarize these texts. Another way is to establish basic semantic links between pictures, find the best matched text, and make necessary text summarization. The establishment of the semantic links relies on the relations between their tags determined by the existing texts, semantic links and the categories of pictures.

(2) *Selecting one picture to represent a set of related pictures.* A solution is to transform this issue into a text summarization issue: Transform pictures into texts according to the way described in (1), summarize the texts, and then select a picture to represent the summary by matching its tags and the core words of the summary.

(3) *Generating a small network of pictures from a large set of related pictures.* A solution is to establish the semantic links between pictures, discover the communities of the semantic link network of pictures, select one picture to represent one community, and construct a network of the representative pictures.

(4) *Generating a small network of texts according to a large set of pictures.* A solution is to discover the communities of the semantic link network of pictures, to select one text to represent one community according to the tags of pictures within the community, and to construct a semantic link network of the representative texts.

A solution to implement this idea is to make use of existing summaries made by humans and the corresponding pictures in the networks of pictures, tags, summaries, source texts and people who were involved in forming and using these things.

The key problem is to select a better picture from the candidates that have the same projections on the dimensions of time, location and topic, because the semantic links between pictures may be poor. For example, it is difficult to automatically find the abstraction relationship between pictures. Modern cameras can generate pictures with time and location information, so the summarization of pictures can be carried out in a space of four dimensions: *language, feature, time* and *location*.

An interesting work is the interpretation of paintings. Different from pictures, paintings represent observations of artists in painting languages. Paintings can be interpreted through formalising the painting languages, recognising the components of the painting, constructing a semantic link network of the components, and clustering components and paintings according to existing categories, themes, authors and types of painting, and mapping the semantic link network into the historical backgrounds of the paintings including the events that the painting represented and the characteristics of the artists.

General framework of summarization

13

Humans have been pursuing the ways to represent thoughts, emotions and thoughts. Various devices and approaches have been invented and developed to represent and process different forms such as natural language representations, pictures, videos and graphs. Various representations constitute a representation space with particular structure and operations. Summarization is a kind of operation that inputs one or more representations and then outputs a new representation.

13.1 Unification

Let us recall how human representations are generated through different channels. People have the following common experience: Scanning the symbols within text (e.g., novel) generates some images in the mind, and the images emerge before symbols when recalled. Similar images will be generated when seeing the movie about the novel. A distinguished characteristic is that humans generate a semantic image (including mental behaviors) different from the input. This indicates that the *human mind uniformly processes various things at a certain cognitive level.* This indicates the possibility of creating a unified method for processing different objects such as texts, pictures, videos and graphs.

Cognitive psychologists argue that people usually remember meaning rather than exact representation and that meaning is represented through the perceptual and motor systems for interacting with the world. The categorical organization of knowledge strongly influences the way to encode and remember experiences [6]. This is the psychological basis of categorization.

Humans represent what they have seen or felt as semantic images in the mental space through interacting and experiencing in the physical space, and summarizing representations and revising representations during communicating with each other in social space where motivations are generated. To facilitate communication, humans indicate the mental semantic images in the language commonly used in society, but it is difficult to communicate in the form of what they have seen or felt. A semantic image can be regarded as a semantic link network of concepts, which contains rich features and operations.

Discovering unity in diversity is a scientific research method that has generated many important scientific principles and theories, for example, Maxwell successfully unified electricity and magnetism. However, unifying different theories is difficult because it needs to uncover the common nature behind existing theories, and different theories may represent different aspects of a domain and use different

Multi-Dimensional Summarization in Cyber-Physical Society. DOI: http://dx.doi.org/10.1016/B978-0-12-803455-2.00013-5

representation systems that are difficult to be unified. Sometimes, pursuing unity is an adventure like the pursuit of the unified field theory.

Knowledge representation approaches such as the production rule [27], the frame [81] and the semantic net [97] are symbol systems that can carry out reasoning for solving problems. A unified representation should reflect the most fundamental characteristics of the concerned representations. The Unified Modeling Language (UML) is an attempt to uniformly represent business processes and behaviors, software architectures, processes, behaviors, and data structures.

Establishing a unified representation enables a summarization system to uniformly process various representations. A transformational development of the fundamental infrastructure of cyberspace (e.g., a new generation computer) and smarter devices will influence the generation of new representations.

13.2   Transformation with dimension reduction

A text can be transformed into a semantic link network of language units of different granularities such as words, sentences and paragraphs. One semantic link network of language units can further link to the other semantic link networks of language units to form a larger semantic link network.

A video can also be transformed into a semantic link network of video clips. Links between words in subtitles and video clips can be established. Links between videos are enriched through the mediation of words. For the videos with scripts, words will play more important roles in representing videos. In addition, voice and music can render the link between videos.

A unified method for summarizing different forms can be developed by transforming texts, videos, pictures and graphs into semantic link networks of forms. A complex semantic link network of different forms enables one form (e.g., movies) to link to the other forms (e.g., novels, scripts, pictures of actors and actresses, posters, comments, related movies, etc.). The form of a summary can be a small semantic link network of texts, videos, audios, pictures and graphs, which provides more semantic indicators than a single type of form like a silent movie. Appropriate coordination between different forms concerns humanity and sociology. The scale of a summary depends on user requirement and cognitive level.

Cyberspace consists of huge links between texts, videos, audios, pictures and graphs, corresponding to human senses and the structures of cyberspace, physical space and social space. Texts, videos, audios, pictures or graphs do not exist independently. Explicit or implicit links between them form complex representations. One form of representation like text usually links to the other forms of representation like pictures, and possibly to videos, audios and graphs, which can be regarded as citations for explanation, complementation or extension. The network evolved with social interactions determines different summaries at different times.

Transformation between representations is a way to realize unification. It inputs one form of representation and outputs another form of representation. Summarization is a special transformation that operates dimension reduction for easier understanding.

From this point of view, summarization can be regarded as a transformation of reducing the dimensions of a representation so that the dimensions of representation can be linked to and merge with the dimensions in the mental space of the persons who require the summary. Therefore, we have the following definition.

Definition (Multi-dimensional summarization): Multi-dimensional summarization is a function $S(P(X_1, \ldots, X_m)) = T(X_i, \ldots, X_j)$, which transforms any representation $p(X_1 = p_1 \ldots, X_m = p_m)$ in the source space of representations P *with* dimensions $X_1, \ldots,$ *and* X_m into a representation $t(X_i = t_i, \ldots, X_j = p_j)$ in the target space of representations T *with dimensions* $X_i, \ldots,$ *and* X_j $(m \geq j \geq i \geq 1)$ such that t contains the core of p at dimensions $X_i, \ldots,$ *and* X_j.

The dimensions of P vary with different sources and the dimensions of T vary with the readers of the summary. Some relations may exist between dimensions. Usually, T has a small number of dimensions. The scale of summary can be regarded as a dimension. The reason is that a reader can easily and quickly understand the summary if the dimension of the target space is the same as the dimension of the reader's personal space, which represents the reader's cognitive architecture.

The definition of summarization based on citation gives the range of T, and $(X_i, \ldots, X_j)$ reflects the basic cognitive level of readers. As discussed before, a dimension represents computing that inputs a set of representations and then outputs a category hierarchy.

The transformation with dimension reduction unveils the nature of general summarization. One of the significant applications of transformation with dimension reduction is query-based summarization. It enables a summarization to generate different summaries from the same source according to the interests of users.

13.3   Cognitive level

Cognitive psychologists have been exploring mental concepts through rational definition, prototype, exemplar and knowledge studies. They try to find the basic cognitive level in the concept hierarchy shared by people [83]. However, different communities can have different cognitive levels. The basic cognitive level can be established for the hierarchy of universal concepts. The cyberspace including the Wikipedia is reflecting more and more of the hierarchy of the universal concepts. The cognitive hierarchy of different communities corresponds to different subgraphs of the hierarchy and has different basic cognitive levels. The cognitive level for a particular research field can be reflected by all of its papers. It stands for the basic cognitive level of all authors in the field.

Relevant research concerns common sense, knowledge level, and abstraction [82,88,118]. Physical instruments such as functional magnetic resonance imaging fMRI and electroencephalography EGG have been used to detect the physical status of mind [120]. The relations between language and brain have attracted many researchers [12,37].

Cognitive level distinguishes the understandability of readers. It also determines the appropriate depth of the dimensions of the representation space that can convey the contents of the author to the reader.

A summary is suitable if its cognitive level is the same as the reader's cognitive level.

The following are some rules to make a suitable summary:

(1) *If the cognitive level of the original representation is the same as the reader's cognitive level, the summary should use the representations indicating the core in the original representation.*

(2) *If the cognitive level of the original representation is higher than the reader's cognitive level, the summary should use more specific concepts in the category hierarchy of common sense.*

(3) *If the cognitive level of the original representation is lower than the reader's cognitive level, the summary should use more general concepts within the category hierarchy of common sense.*

13.4   Representation lattice

In psychology, representation is a kind of hypothetical internal cognitive symbol that represents external reality. Externalization of the internal representation involves complex mental, physical and social behaviors. Ontology helps establish a general representation of the nature of the world, knowledge and knowing. From the pragmatism point of view, ontology was developed by IT professionals for information sharing [5,50]. Ontology helps explain representation and establish the links between representations. This enables summarization systems to use more general or more specific concepts in summary.

Representations can be generalized, united, categorized and semantically linked to form a lattice of representations at a cognitive level of ontology as shown in Figure 13.1. A cognitive level determines a representation lattice rather than one

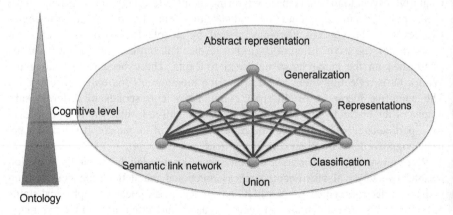

Figure 13.1 Representation lattice at certain cognitive level.

concept. Operations on representations enrich the structure of the lattice. Abstraction and analogy are the important operations of generating representations [139−141].

Abstract representation reflects the common characteristics of a set of different types of concerned representations. Abstract representation is particularly useful for developing theories. Mathematical tools such as logic, algebra and graphs can help develop abstract representations. However, overly abstract representation may be insignificant in real applications.

The union of representations integrates different representations to provide a global view of these representations. It is important to ensure the understandability and expressiveness of the integrated representation. As a kind of union, data integration enables users to get a global view of data generated from different sources [38,53,68]. The union of the semantic link network and the category space is a way to form a semantic space. The multi-dimensional categorization space and semantic linking network were used to represent and organize semantic images. Different representations of the same thing can be linked to the same semantic image for understanding and thinking [139−141].

The general summarization inputs a representation and a cognitive level at a certain category hierarchy and then outputs a representation lattice and a recommended representation.

13.5 Display

The basic problem of displaying a summary is how to determine the display features such as the location and the size of its representation components within the given screen size. The following is a process of display:

(1) Divide the display area into k scopes, e.g., core, close-core, relevant-to-core and peripheral, and determine k different sizes of displaying components within the k scopes according to the number of components and the size of the screen.
(2) Determine the core representation(s), put the core representation(s) into the current scope with $size = 1$ (maximum).
(3) Select the representations close to the representations within the current scope, and evenly put them into the next scope with a smaller size $size = k + 1$.
(4) Do (3) until $size > k$.

Different sizes can be used to display different representations within the same scope according to their importance. Different colors can be used to differentiate scopes. People with different culture may have different preferences to color. According to the nations of readers, colors can be selected more appropriately to enable the core scope to have the most attractive color. One more dimension needs to be considered when determining the scopes and the sizes if a three-dimensional screen is selected.

The discussion of the general framework of summarization is also suitable for big data research, including summarization and visualization.

Summarization of things in Cyber-Physical Society

14

It is estimated that 24—50 billion devices will be connected to the Internet by 2020. With the rapid development of the Internet of Things, cyberspace is connected to the physical space and social space. Bigger data are being generated in addition to the big data generated in social media, the Web, mobile devices, and organization. How to summarize the big data to provide appropriate on-demand services and predictive suggestions for humans is a challenge.

14.1 Cyber-Physical Society

Cyber-Physical Society is a complex space that generates and evolves diverse subspaces to contain different types of individuals interacting with, reflecting or influencing each other directly or indirectly through the cyber, physical, socio and mental subspaces. Versatile individuals and socio roles coexist harmoniously yet evolve, provide appropriate on-demand information, knowledge and services for each other, transform from one form into another, interact with each other through various links, and self-organize according to socio value chains. It ensures healthy and meaningful lives of individuals, and maintains a reasonable rate of expansion of individuals in light of overall capacity and the material, knowledge, and service flow cycles [140]. Human-Machine-Nature Symbiosis is a basic relation that can help realize the harmonious development of Cyber-Physical Society. A detailed discussion is given in Appendix A.

Cyber-Physical Society not only consists of cyberspace and the physical space but also social space that holds humans, knowledge, society and culture. It is a future interconnection environment that connects the nature, cyberspace and society with certain principles and rules. Research on Cyber-Physical Society will lead to the transformation of science and technology. Investigating computing in Cyber-Physical Society will lead to the transformation of computing paradigm.

Humans consciously and subconsciously establish various links, emerge semantic images and reason in mind, learn linking effect and rules, select linked individuals to interact, and form closed loops through links while co-experiencing in multiple spaces in a lifetime. Machines are limited in these abilities although various graph-based models have been used to link resources in the cyberspace. The following are the fundamental limitations of machine intelligence:

(1) Machines know few links and rules in the physical space, physiological space, psychological space, socio space and mental space, so it is unrealistic to expect machines to discover laws and problems in these spaces.

Multi-Dimensional Summarization in Cyber-Physical Society. DOI: http://dx.doi.org/10.1016/B978-0-12-803455-2.00014-7

(2) Machines can only follow pre-designed algorithms and data structures to process data in the cyberspace. They are limited in ability to go beyond the cyberspace, to learn linking rules, to know the effect of linking, and to explain computing results according to physical, physiological, psychological and socio laws.

Linking various spaces will create a complex space. Diverse spaces will emerge, evolve, compete and cooperate with each other to extend machine intelligence and human intelligence to cyber-physical-socio intelligence with multi-disciplinary revolution. Exploration will go beyond previous ideals on intelligence and computing.

14.2 The necessity of investigating summarization in Cyber-Physical Society

The following applications request to move summarization beyond cyberspace:

(1) *Summarizing history.* Modern history is being reflected by a complex network of artifacts in the physical space and the big data, including texts, graphs, pictures, videos, audios and other forms of media in cyberspace. The method for constructing, coordinating and managing the complex network of humans and various representations, as well as the method for analyzing the patterns in the network through time are essential to the summarization of history.

(2) *Summarizing events.* Human organs can sense events from multiple channels and emerge semantic images in mind. Human summarization is to summarize the semantic images and represent the summary in language. Automatic summarization of events such as conferences or discussions need to collect various representations generated from social networks in cyberspace and physical features such as location and temperature in the physical space through various sensors. Data collected by sensor networks and the summaries of pictures, videos and sounds provide the basis for summarizing events.

(3) *Summarizing behaviors.* The management of a smart city needs the support from the big data on human behaviors sensed from the cyber-physical city and various temporal social events. Summaries of patients' behaviors sensed through smart rooms can help doctors analyze the symptom of the patients.

(4) *Summarizing thoughts.* Humans invent and use languages to externalize thoughts in mind. Scientists' thoughts are reflected by evolving citation networks of publications. Summarizing thoughts in scientific papers is significant in tracing and analyzing the development of research areas and inspiring new research. Research concerns the collection of all publications of one or a group of scientists published through time and all follow-up citations, and the analysis of the formation process of thoughts through the citation network. Enabling scientific papers to link text to the objects in cyberspace, physical space and social space can accurately and vividly represent scientific thoughts [140]. Symbolic language is hard to accurately represent thought, so the summarization of scientific thoughts should go beyond text into these spaces.

(5) *Summarization as learning.* Summarization has become a way of learning because humans are limited in time and energy to gain knowledge from reading the rapidly expanding original resources in the form of texts, pictures, videos and tables of data; and humans are also limited in knowledge to learn knowledge of other disciplines. In a learning organization, people often play the role of summarizers, which enables members to

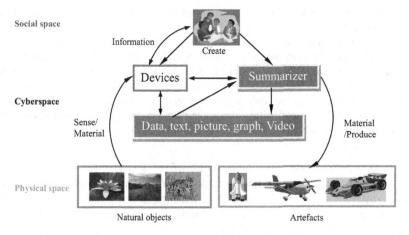

Figure 14.1 The diversity of summarization in Cyber-Physical Society.

learn knowledge in a short time. A good member of a learning organization can select the appropriate materials with motivation and consideration of the existing knowledge structure of the members, and can represent the summary in the common language of the community. To have this skill of summarization is a challenge to automatic summarization research.

As shown in Figure 14.1, a summarizer can not only generate data, text, picture, graph, video and the combinations of different types of data, but can also generate the physical objects through a production process.

14.3   Representation and interaction in Cyber-Physical Society

A cyber-physical-social representation is a process of forming structure and semantics in a multi-dimensional representation space. The following are some general dimensions:

(1) Representations at the physical dimension are based on physical features, measures, rules and principles.
(2) Representations at the biological dimension are based on biological features, measures, rules, and principles.
(3) Representations at the language dimension are based on language features, measures and rules like grammar and idioms. Language can be in diverse forms such as symbolic natural language and film language.
(4) Representations at the social dimension are based on social features, measures, rules and principles such as values, social relations, regulations, rules and strategies.
(5) Representations in the mental space are semantic images [139,140]. New semantic images can be generated with operating semantic images such as abstraction and fusion. Abstract semantic images such as country, people and dragon do not directly reflect the

physical objects. Some abstract semantic images are only rendered by symbols and operations. When studying languages, links between symbols and semantic images are established in minds. When writing, symbols emerge to represent semantic images. While reading, semantic images are rebuilt through links between symbols and semantic images. Some semantic images can be generalized as knowledge including concepts, commonsense, principles, rules and methods. Knowledge grows and self-organizes through understanding, speaking, listening, writing and reading. Ideally, a summary can match the readers' mental status—the active points in the readers' mental space reflecting the real-time interest. However, the real-time mental statuses of readers are not directly accessible.

Human representation space includes all of the above dimensions. This determines the difference between human understanding and machine operation. There may be different mappings from one representation at one dimension into the other representation at the other dimension, so a representation can be understood through multiple projections at some dimensions.

Different individuals experience and learn independently. Therefore, different individuals may emerge different semantic images about the same thing. Representation and understanding are involved in the process of organizing language elements with intension. A representation is understood only when its semantic image emerges in the minds of a community of practice and links to the existing semantic images.

Figure 14.2 depicts the scenario of representation and interaction in the complex space of cyberspace, physical space and social space. People can communicate with each other and interact with various physical objects through the physical space interface according to physical features, measures, rules and principles, with people and artifacts through social space interface according to social features, measures, rules and principles; and with various digital resources through cyberspace interface according to cyber features, measures, rules and principles when representing and interacting. For example, people can search the Web and send/receive email, talk to friends, and feel the real world (force, velocity, taste, smell, emotion, etc.) to get necessary information, experience, help, and various services with social motivation

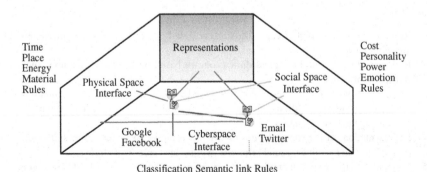

Figure 14.2 Representation and interaction in Cyber-Physical Society.

when living, studying, and working (writing research proposals, doing online business, etc.).

Interaction in one space may have influence in another space, but the measures, rules and principles in one space are usually not suitable for another space due to the difference of the natural features of the existence and interaction unless commonality can be found. Frequent interaction can not only distract attention and thinking but also damage health (e.g., many people are addicted to online group chat), so appropriately coordinating various interactions is important for creative work, effective study and wellbeing.

14.4 Principles

From the view of physical dimension, representation behaviors such as writing and reading consume material and energy, therefore follow the physical laws and principles like physical movement. Because of the limitation of energy consumption and lifetime, humans tend to behave with less time and lower energy consumption in both large-scale and small-scale. This is also in line with the cognitive economy—the tendency of minimizing effort and resources in cognitive processes [22].

Efficiency Principle: *Humans behave consciously or unconsciously with lower consumption of energy and time.*

This determines the following principle of behaviors in Cyber-Physical Society.

Cyber-Physical-Social Locality: *Human psychological system tends to behave within a smaller space in the cyberspace, physical space and social space, where time is a common dimension.*

The following observations explain the above two principles:

(1) Humans write words sequentially within a limited physical region, which is determined by the physiological structure of organs, especially eyes, arms, etc.
(2) Eyes sense sentences within one paragraph more directly and efficiently than in a larger area as the physical structure enables eyes to view only a small region. Therefore, sentences in one paragraph can represent knowledge and be understood more efficiently.
(3) An appropriate size of a paragraph helps memorization more efficiently than larger size. Clearly, readers spend more time to remember such a paragraph occupying one page or several pages, and much more time will be spent to memorize a book without paragraphs. The appropriate size varies with the reading skills of readers but there is an appropriate size for a particular reader.
(4) Transformation from sense to memorization and transformation from memorization to understanding consume time.

A psychological space for understanding may be determined by the cyber-physical-social locality as it significantly influences behaviors. Figure 14.3 depicts

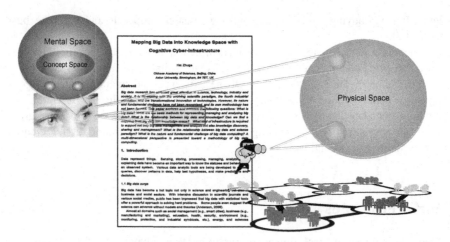

Figure 14.3 The locality of behaviors in cyber-physical-social space.

the locality of various behaviors in the cyber-physical-social space, e.g., scanning text, observing the physical space while standing at a social network, social networking, representing observations as concepts in the mental space, and linking concepts. The category space links the sense from the cyberspace (e.g., reading a paper) to the sense of observing the physical space.

The above principles indicate the following lemmas.

Lemma: *Components of the same representation are relevant representations.*

For example, sentences in the same paragraph are relevant representations, as they render the same meaning and are understood as a whole while reading. Two sentences in different paragraphs can also be related if they are about the same concept in the category hierarchy.

Rules of relevancy: The relevancy depends on specific relations like co-occurrence, which is a kind of weak relevancy. The following are some rules of relevancy.

(1) *Representations are relevant to each other if they are relevant to the same representation or close representations.* The representation can be in the original text or in other texts, can be in other forms such as picture, video, and concept.
(2) *Representations that cite the same representation are relevant citations.*
(3) *Representations that cite the same representation are relevant representations.*
(4) *A representation cited by many representations probably renders the core, and the more citations the higher the probability.*

With respect to reading, the characteristics of eye movements, perceptual span, integration of information across saccades, eye movement control, and individual differences were discussed in psychology [66,101,102].

14.5   Personality

Humans leave some subtle personality in representations, including texts. Knowing personalities enables more accurate summarization, and can also help a summarization system to make on-demand recommendations and predict abnormal behaviors so as to provide necessary help. Psychologists have made great efforts to find psychological states by analyzing texts [44,93,114]. Current online social networks such as Blogs and Twitter can facilitate those efforts with more personalized texts and link to more people. So, personality is a dimension of summarization. Coordinating representations in cyberspace, physical space and social space enables a summarization system to reflect more subtle traces.

Humans have been inventing and using various devices that can record human traces. Some devices are able to capture and identify facial expression and gesture expression, which can also be used to reflect personality [54]. Mobile phones are widely used to take pictures, record voices and videos, and get locations that hold physical objects and relate behaviours and events. Smart wearable devices such as smart watches and Google glasses will be able to measure physiological features and local environment more accurately. Representation in the personality dimension is technologically feasible. New technologies for collecting information in the physical space and the social space significantly influence the form of representation.

Limitations and challenges

15

The limitation of summarization lies in the natural differences between human and machine, between languages, and between the ways of observation and thinking of authors and those of readers. The significant evolution of documents in form and function in cyber-physical society challenges the paradigm of summarization research.

15.1 Limitations of automatic summarization

The ability to make summarizations reflects human intelligence. Human can summarize things according to motivation, observation, experience, knowledge, and the management of change. Human summarization can be creative, e.g., in generating new ideas according to facts, discovering new physical laws through summarizing phenomena, and generating methodologies, scientific theories and philosophical thoughts according to phenomena. Humans also have limitations, for example, in time, energy and abilities for reading the constantly expanding ocean of texts.

Automatic summarization can play a certain role in making routine summarization in narrow areas, for example, automatically making a draft "related work" or surveying large-scale papers in a certain area for scientific research according to the given theme. However, automatic summarization systems do not have minds (with experience and knowledge), physiological characteristics, and social characteristics as humans do, so it is not realistic to expect machines to generate a fluent, exciting, or inspiring summary through predefined algorithms. On the other hand, the designers of the algorithms for summarization have limitations in knowing the thought of the authors and the interests of readers, so they are unable to design an ideal general-purpose summarizer. This implies that automatically generating a human-level summary is the limitation of automatic summarization. This can be the test for the intelligence of machines like Turing test:

A summarization system reaches a certain level of human intelligence if a certain portion of users with a certain level of education cannot distinguish the summary of a text made by a person with the same level of education as the readers and the summary generated from the same text by the summarization system.

Currently, an automatic summarizer can be easily distinguished from a human summarizer.

Limitation also lies in the big gap between the representations processed by machines in cyberspace and the representations used by humans who share knowledge with each other and obtain experience not only in cyberspace but also in the physical space and social space. It is still hard for nonprofessional people to communicate with machines and to understand the functions and principles of the system. This involves language and understanding issues.

Multi-Dimensional Summarization in Cyber-Physical Society. DOI: http://dx.doi.org/10.1016/B978-0-12-803455-2.00015-9

Human have created different tools and languages to represent the complex world, but it is hard to represent a complex system in just one language. The transformation from one representation into the other will lose information. For example, translating a Chinese novel into English and translating a Chinese ink painting into oil painting. This is one of the natural limitations of summarization.

15.2 Active documents

Documents are evolving in cyberspace, from language-intensive to multi-media, and from passive and read-only into interactive. Some documents have background systems that control interactions. For example, Wikipedia has a version-control mechanism to manage the contents edited by different contributors. Microsoft Word can check the spelling errors in real time, remind writers of possible errors, and help correct obvious errors in some cases. Active X is a Microsoft technology that allows users to view and edit Microsoft Word, Excel, and PDF documents inside Web browsers. Application-oriented active documents are desirable in the future Cyber-Physical Society.

A primitive framework of active document was proposed in [133]. An active document framework was defined as a self-representable, self-explainable, and self-executable document mechanism. The self-explanation ability is based on the reasoning function. The granularity hierarchy, template hierarchy, background knowledge and semantic links between fragments reflect the content of document. A set of built-in engines is responsible for browsing, retrieving and reasoning, which can work in a way best suited to the content of document. Besides browsing and retrieval services, the active document supports intelligent information services such as complex question answering, e-learning, and assistant problem solving. The client side service provider is responsible for the retrieval of the required active document while the detailed information services are provided by the background document mechanism.

Human reading behaviors have changed from reading language-intensive pages to hyperlinked pages with intensive headings, pictures, and videos. This change significantly influences the way of understanding and requirements for summarization. The paradigm of research is faced with a shift in the evolution of documents because research objects have changed and ways of reading have significantly changed.

15.3 Challenges

A strategy to break the limitations is to create a new computing architecture. Recently, IBM researchers developed an efficient chip, TrueNorth, inspired by the function of the human brain. It is reported that its architecture is different from the von Neumann architecture. Each core integrates memory, computation, and communication. In the future, machines will be able to simulate more brain functions, but it is still difficult to bridge the gap between low-level functions (e.g., neural-level functions) and high-level intelligence like summarization.

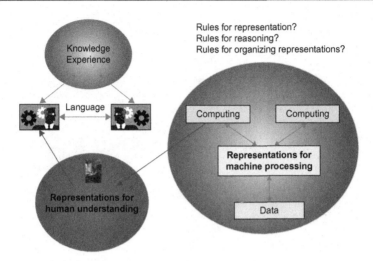

Figure 15.1 Computing with the representations for human understanding.

Another strategy to improve current research with texts is to incorporate pictures, videos, and graphs in summaries to enable different forms of representations to enforce each other as discussed. It is important to explore the common rules in summarizing different objects and in different applications. To facilitate understanding, a new interface for representing the summary of different objects needs to be explored.

Further, there's a goal to build a human-machine-nature symbiotic environment, where humans and machines interact and complement each other in the physical space and social space. The challenge to do this is to provide necessary summarization at the real time of thinking. To achieve this goal, a summarization system needs to know users' cognitive levels, psychological statuses, and personality.

Traditional computing is to design algorithms that transform input into output, which are formally represented by humans so that both machines and humans can easily understand the meaning of the representations. One of the challenges of computing is that the representation of the input and the representation of the output are not suitable for both machines and human. The semantics of the representations is usually undetermined. For text summarization, the representation of the input and the representation of the output are in natural language, which is hard to be accurately specified. Machines process symbols according to some predetermined constraints and rules without understanding the meaning of representations. Therefore, it is difficult for machines to generate a summary that is suitable for humans to read. Appropriately representing computing results can be a part of solving problems. From this point of view, the limitation of computing is the limitation of those constraints and rules. The way to break the limitation is to learn the rules on the semantics of input and output. As depicted in Figure 15.1, the challenge of computing for the representation of human understanding is to discover the rules for representation, reasoning, and organizing representations.

Creative summarization

16

Creative summarization is based on knowledge, including common sense, knowledge of language use, and the knowledge to be represented. The key is to transform various representations (e.g., text) into knowledge through information modelling, and cognitive modelling, and then transform knowledge into representation (summary) through information modelling.

16.1 Unconventional mapping

The key to simulate a human summarization process is to map the external representation into knowledge. However, it is difficult to make a direct mapping through a single closed computing process because of the limitations of the predefined computing processes, closed systems, and the knowledge of the designers [139].

A solution is to divide the problem of the unconventional mapping into three sub-problems, conquer these sub-problems (by establishing submappings), and then integrate the solutions (submappings) into a complex mapping (an interactive computing model). Figure 16.1 depicts an interactive system of mapping representation (e.g., text) into knowledge through an interactive system consisting of information modeling, cognition modeling, and knowledge space modeling. The system can also map knowledge into a summary.

The following sections introduce the information modeling system, cognition modeling system, and knowledge space modeling system in detail.

16.2 Information modeling

The basic viewpoint of information modeling is that information of a representation can only be generated through a process of representation such as writing and reading. A static representation itself does not generate information. Information generates and evolves through a representation process or a group of representation processes that interact with each other. Although the result of representation may be the same, different processes could generate different information, which may be lost in final representation. Mapping the processes into a category space is the basic step for interpreting information.

16.2.1 Main functions

Different information models could generate different information from the same representation. To model various representations of data, an information modeling

Multi-Dimensional Summarization in Cyber-Physical Society. DOI: http://dx.doi.org/10.1016/B978-0-12-803455-2.00016-0

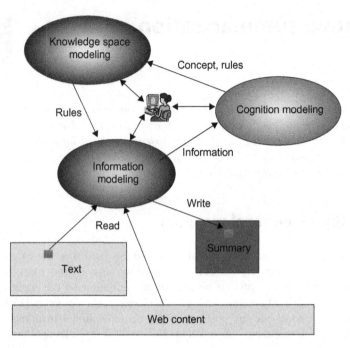

Figure 16.1 Unconventional mapping through an interactive complex system.

system needs to ensure the diversity of models, which represent different under-standings and satisfy different application requirements of applications.

The information modeling system transforms various data like texts into infor-mation by making use of computing models and by measuring the function of time and interest (e.g., the measure of information quantity in text as discussed in [18]). The system can also transform information into text(s) through an appropriate com-puting model such as a writing process. The current computing models on texts like TF-IDF and topic model needs additional space for interpretation.

Various information modeling methods can be developed to model the information in text. For example, a text scanning mechanism was proposed for generating the dynamic impressions of words in text by simulating the recall process, association process, and forget process during reading [129]. The interpretation of the impression needs an interpretation space.

To simulate human observation characteristics, an observation scope of reading and writing can be used to dynamically generate information within a certain scale through writing and reading process. For text representations, the scale can refer to a word, phrase, sentence, paragraph, and text. The observation scope provides a mechanism for simulating writing and reading. Different traces of moving the observation scope represent different ways of understandings.

The information modeling system can also input the rules from human or from the knowledge space to guide information modeling. It can also coordinate multiple models to make use of the combined advantages of different models. The observation scope can zoom in and zoom out through different dimensions when scanning to generate the information of different scales according to the rules.

16.2.2   Generation of interest space

The interest space generates and evolves with various interactions in the physical space and social space. The physical objects that people interact with have social characteristics. People have various interests in the physical objects, assigned specific meanings to some objects within specific communities (e.g., using different flowers to symbolize different meanings), and leave impressions in minds. These impressions become interests when they are linked to the psychological meaning of life. The combination of different physical objects is a complex representation of interest. Artists often use the combination of colors and the combination of the physical objects to represent interests. Interest is more natural, intuitive, and simple while motivation is more social, proactive, and complex.

Interests have representations in long-term memory and have impressions in the category space. Some interests have a higher intention aspect than others. Writers and readers tend to focus on the higher interest to save time, enjoy writing and reading, and to inspire thinking. Interests can change with the generation of new impressions through interaction. Several interests can be composed into a complex interest in the interest space.

The complete modeling of interest needs a multi-dimensional cyber-physical space to measure the interest representations in different spaces. Incorporating the psychological views into the multi-dimensional category space discussed in Chapter 5, Multi-dimensional methodology, a high-level interest space can be formed as shown in the left hand part of Figure 16.2, which mainly consists of the following dimensions:

(1) *Time*.
(2) *Need*, which consists of the following two coordinates:
   (a) *Basic need*, which consists of *physiological need*, *safety*, and *love*.
   (b) *Social need*, which consists of *esteem*, *self-actuation*, and *belonging*.
(3) *Recognition*, which consists of the following two coordinates:
   (a) *Accomplishment*.
   (b) *Linkage*.

More dimensions of the high-level interest space can be constructed by selecting different levels of the meaning of life [71], and validating the relations between the dimensions according to the criteria of a space. However, it is too general to be a personal interest space. A personal interest space consists of some special dimensions like sport. Some personal interests can be discovered from observing behaviors like writing and reading.

With the assumptions of the meaning-of-life hierarchy in psychology and the category hierarchy, a personal interest space can be automatically generated through the following steps, as depicted in Figure 16.2.

(1) Constructing a high-level interest space by selecting the levels from the hierarchy of the meaning of life and constructing the space according to the criteria of structuring a space.

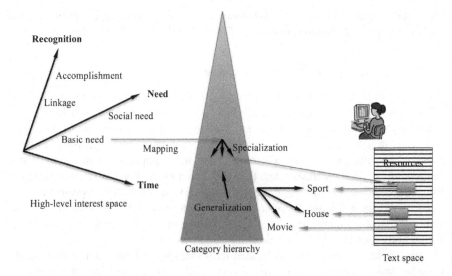

Figure 16.2 Automatic generation of interest space from text space: extending the high-level interest space through top-down specialization, dimension extraction, and bottom-up generalization.

(2) Selecting a dimension from the high-level interest space.

(3) Mapping the dimensions into the category hierarchy to specialize the dimensions.

(4) Identifying the interested representations in the text space according to the behaviors of writing and reading, for example, writing blogs and clicking hyperlinks.

(5) Mapping the interested representations into the category hierarchy to make generalization bottom-up towards the dimensions of the high-level interest space.

(6) Identifying a tree of categories in the category hierarchy.

(7) Verifying whether the extension satisfies the criteria of structuring the space or not.

(8) If the tree satisfies the criteria, linking the tree of categories to a coordinate of one dimension at the high-level interest space.

(9) Go to (2) until all dimensions have been extended or a pre-determined condition is satisfied.

The approach to automatically extracting dimensions and constructing a multi-dimensional space discussed in Chapter 5, Multi-dimensional methodology, can apply to the establishment of the interest space.

16.2.3 Interest-led reading model

The information human obtained from reading text is different from the existing computing models that scan text words by words. Human reading is often interest-led, which can quickly locate the interested parts within text. It can be used to summarize text according to reader interest.

The following is the basic assumption for interest-led reading. Without this assumption, it will be difficult for humans to quickly identify the interested representations within text without scanning the whole text, and we cannot explain the phenomenon of human's quick reading.

Assumption (predict before reading): *An experienced reader often generated a prediction-of-interest distribution within representation (e.g., text) before reading a new representation (e.g., text).*

The ability to make this prediction is gained from previous reading experience. The person with richer reading experience has a stronger ability to make the prediction. A child without any reading experience does not have the ability of prediction.

The special structure of texts like research papers help people to quickly build the experience. For example, experienced researchers can quickly locate the section that introduces the method, experiment, or result according to their current interests. For researchers on the same topic can even quickly locate the formulas, figures or experiments they are interested in (e.g., for making comparison with their current work).

Is the experience for making this prediction relevant to the organization of the contents read previously? This needs careful verification for human minds.

However, it is certain that a computing system can quickly locate the interest contents if the organization of the contents reflects the structure of text.

In cyberspace, digital documents have built-in indexes to help people quickly access the interested contents. Some software systems even provide a navigation function to help people browse large-scale texts. The influence of reading in cyberspace indicates the following proposition:

Proposition: *Readers who often read traditional representations (e.g., texts) and the representations in cyberspace (e.g., Web pages) tend to build separate experience structures in minds to make prediction for interest-led reading.*

This proposition of separation is in line with the self-observation from reading texts and browsing web pages, for example, people can often point mouse to the particular location according to such features as the location, front size, color, and title of interested contents before close reading the content of a webpage.

Based on the above assumptions, the model is constructed as follows:

Let T be the representation (e.g., text) to be read and I be an interest representation in an interest space, and there is a set of basic representation units W within T (such as word, phrase and sentence) that reflects interest I. $D(I)$ is a function that generates the distribution of W within T according to I, $D(I) = (location(w_1, I))$; $\ldots$, $location(w_n, I))$. A function $S(w, D(I))$ generates a minimum scope that contains w within T *according to* $D(I)$.

The basic reading process:

(1) Input T and I.
(2) Generate $D(I)$.
(3) Put the representation within $S(w_k, D(I))$ into memory for $k = 1, \ldots, n$.
(4) Output the representations with the reading order.

Figure 16.3 depicts the reading model, where the dots denote the representation units within text, the rectangles denote the scopes of the interested representation units, the arrows denote the reading order, and the dotted arrows denote the representations within other texts for a set of texts.

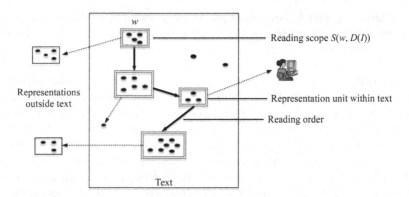

Figure 16.3 The interest-focus reading model, which enables the reading mechanism to focus on the interested parts.

The accompanying processes.

(1) *Memorize*. The current representation is memorized in the short-term memory and then transformed into the long-term memory that can be simulated by a network of categories.

(2) *Recall*. The existing representations in the long-term memory will be reactivated in response to the coming of the new representation.

(3) *Association*. The new representations are linked to the existing representations. As the consequence of association, this will enhance the memory. The association effect is a basic mechanism of human memory. The effect is strong within local range and weak within global range.

(4) *Forget*. Forget is a process of reorganizing memory. A representation's global impression gradually fades out if it does not be recalled for a certain time. The core representations are not easy to fade out because they are often recalled directly or indirectly. The forget speed of a representation depends on its role within the network: (a) One representation closer to the core representations fades out slower. (b) One representation recalled more times fades out slower. (c) One representation with more links will fade out slower.

(5) *Mapping*. Mapping the $S(w_k, D(I))$, $(k = 1, .., n)$ into the category space to get interpretation.

This reading model enables the reading mechanism to focus on the interested scopes. Further, the reading scope inspires associations to expand the scope meaningfully only when the reading mechanism works within the scope. The association can link a representation unit to another representation unit within the text or link to the representation units within the other texts that read before.

The interest-led reading model has the following advantages:

(1) Accurately recommend the interested representations of the text to the reader.
(2) Help readers to understand the text according to interest.
(3) Summarize text according to interest.
(4) Make the multi-media visualization of the interest text by linking the reading scope to images and videos.

The interest-led reading model is in line with the following two propositions:

(1) *The information within text depends not only on text but also on readers.* Reading with different interests generates different information. Therefore, the information of a text is not constant.

(2) *Human can distinguish the interested units from text in a short time,* which is much shorter than recognizing and understanding a representation unit. Humans usually do not remember the uninterested representation units. Long-term memory does not store and operate the uninterested representations.

16.2.4 Three-tier reading assumption

The current knowledge on memory classifies memory as a short-term memory and a long-term memory. The short-term memory may last for only several minutes. However, this assumption cannot explain the following two phenomena:

(1) *Humans can select the interest representation from text in less than a half second while reading a representation, e.g., paragraph.* This means that the speed of selection mechanism can work faster than the short-term memory. The difference of speed implies that the selection mechanism can work independent of the short-term memory.

(2) *Sometimes readers know nothing (or cannot remember) immediately after reading, especially when they are tired or not interested in the reading material.* This implies that some read representations are not transformed into the short-term memory.

The following is a more reasonable assumption:

Assumption: *There exists a mechanism that performs quick scan unconsciously, or there exists a mapping from readers' interests into the representations within text before short-term memory.*

With this assumption, a three-tier reading mechanism can be constructed as follows.

Three-tier reading mechanism: Reading behavior operates with the following three tiers:

(1) *The pre-memory process mechanism scans the text through a reading window, neglects the uninterested representation units, locates the interested representation unit, and forwards the interested representation units to the short-term memory, and continues to scan the text until the end.*

(2) *The short-term memory mechanism stores the interested representation unit, ranks these representation units, and forwards the high-rank representation units to the long-term memory.*

(3) *The long-term memory mechanism emerges relevant representation units in language space and category space, and links the new representation units to the emerging representation units.*

The three-tier reading mechanism is shown in Figure 16.4. The pre-memory processing mechanism scans the text, detects the interest representation according to

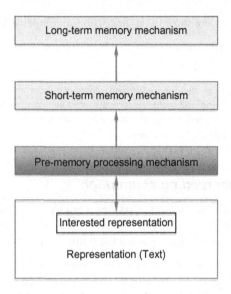

Figure 16.4 Three-tier memory mechanism for interest-led reading.

the features of interest, and forwards the interested part to the short-term memory mechanism. The short-term memory mechanism represents the interest representation and interacts with the long-term memory mechanism to find the links between the current representation and the existing representation in the long-term memory. It forwards the current representation to the long-term memory if there is a link. The long-term memory mechanism maintains the influence of the new representation and the network of representations to support reasoning.

The three-tier assumption interprets why humans can quickly identify the interest representations within text.

16.2.5 Solutions

The interest-led implementation framework is depicted in Figure 16.5. The interest representation I should be operable according to application requests and the rules of operations. If the interest representation is a set of words, the operations are set operations with the mapping between synonyms. A simple location L takes the following form: $L = (a_1/l_1(I), \ldots, a_k/l_k(I))$, where a_1 is the probability of the interest I locating at l_1, and a_k is the probability of interest I locating at l_k, and $a_1 + \ldots + a_k = 1$. Ranks are distributed at locations: $a_1/Rank(representation)@l_1, \ldots, a_k/Rank (Representation)@l_k$.

The following are key steps for implementing an interest-led system.

(1) Formation of the interest-location list, which can be implemented by the following two ways:

    (a) *User definition through interface.* Authors are encouraged to provide a list of interests and the corresponding locations within text when they submit texts (current research

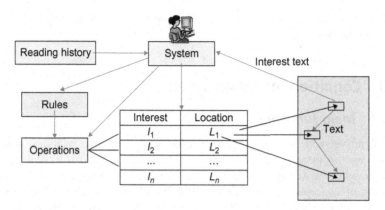

Figure 16.5 The implementation framework for interest-led reading.

paper submission system requests researchers to provide keywords when submitting papers). To realize interest-led reading, the representations where the keywords appeared and the locations are required to list together with the keywords. The list likes the book index that links important subjects or names to the relevant pages (e.g., "scientific method, 32−33, 48"). The interest can be word(s), phrase(s), sentence(s), and other representation forms, so the matching method is needed to find the corresponding representation unit within text. The location of an interest can be the locations of words, phrases, sentences, paragraphs, and sections (or chapters), so a hierarchy of location is needed. This additional work does not spend a lot time of authors.

(b) *Automatic extraction from user reading history*. This way assumes that the users' reading history records are available. The interest list is extracted from user reading history.

  (i) *For Web browsing*, the clicking history on hyperlinks reflects user interest. The hyperlinks on one topic are often clustered within one area of a webpage. For example, the location of the hyperlink "stock market" is fixed on www.sina. com.cn. The users who are interested in it will go directly to the location rather than scanning the page to find the link. So a list of hyperlinks and locations can be established by ranking the clicked hyperlinks and their locations on the web pages according to the click times (e.g., in form of "hyperlink, rank, location").

  (ii) *For traditional texts*, the method for automatically constructing the interest space from texts discussed in Chapter 5, Multi-dimensional methodology, can be used to extend the list to a multi-dimensional space with the locations attached to the interested representations.

(2) The system collects all texts and the lists of interests and the corresponding locations. As authors are also readers, the interest lists represent users interest when the system has many users.

(3) The system finds the relations between interests and locations, e.g., some interests appear at some common locations. A hierarchy of interests can be formed by clustering interests.

(4) Users can represent new interests and the system can generate the corresponding locations according to the existing experience or the operations on the existing experience. If there is no matched experience, the system will scan the text(s) to find the corresponding locations.

(5) The system records the new interest and the corresponding locations if it finds the location. Otherwise it will set up "waiting" status to invite users to give the locations.

(6) The system links the selected representations according to the interest of the user for reading quickly.

16.3 Cognition modeling system

16.3.1 Main functions

The cognitive modeling system is for discovering concepts, relations, and rules through various mental processes including reasoning. It receives information from the information modeling system, forms concepts, and links the concepts to existing networks of concepts with the guide of the high-level concepts, constraints (e.g., time), and motivation. It remembers, recalls, associates, and forgets to evolve the impression of concepts.

A cognitive modeling system works with a conscious system and an unconscious system, which interact and compensate with each other. The conscious system consists of memory management, motivation management, and various reasoning mechanisms (analogical reasoning, inductive reasoning, and deductive reasoning) as well as management and explanation management. The unconscious system mainly consists of forget, implicit association, and meta-cognition mechanisms. The cognitive modeling system can output concepts, relations and rules to the knowledge space modeling system for verification and organization.

The proposition of separating the unconscious system from the conscious system supports the pre-memory assumption.

Meta cognition [86] argues that the cognitive processes concern the meta-level and the object-level. The meta-level contains a dynamic model of the object-level, and the two levels are coordinated through control relation and monitoring relation.

16.3.2 Cognitive reading model

Humans operate their mental space while reading text. Different people can obtain different experiences from reading. People can learn concepts and various links between concepts generated from mental interactions through reading texts. Some people can learn patterns and rules about language use and understanding from reading more and more texts, and from reading more and more texts about a particular domain or of an author.

The skilled readers can quickly identify the locations of the interested representations according to some rules obtained from reading texts. They can also quickly get the meaning of a text by using a certain rules. For example, established researchers of a domain can get the meaning of a new paper quicker than a newcomer because the established researchers have already established concepts and links between concepts indicated as words in the paper and thus saves time of understanding.

Figure 16.6 depicts the cognitive reading model, which consists of a set of mental operations on the cognitive mechanism. The cognitive mechanism consists of

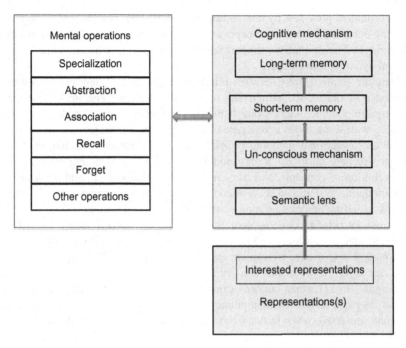

Figure 16.6 A cognitive reading model.

long-term memory, short-term memory, the unconscious mechanism, and a semantic lens, which locates a scope within the text with zoom-in and zoom-out
functions.

16.4 Knowledge space modeling system

The knowledge space modeling system consists of several self-contained knowledge systems and mappings between systems. It has structure, operations, rules, and
reasoning mechanisms. It verifies the input (concepts, relations, or rules) provided
by the cognitive modeling system. If an input can be proved by existing knowledge,
the knowledge space accepts the input as knowledge. Otherwise the system rejects
the input. Its structure can be modeled by a lattice consisting of the high-level general concepts (the top level reflects the worldview) and the low-level basic concepts, which indicates a particular category of knowledge. Some concepts are priori
while others are posteriori. Humans create the priori concepts, which supervise
learning and the classification of posteriori concepts. The middle-level concepts are
the specialization of the high-level concepts and the generalization of the low-level
concepts. The structure of the lattice can be enriched through analyzing the open
Web contents like Wikipedia and the existing ontologies, which indicate popular
categories, inheriting a concept, and enriching it as the middle-level concepts by

the information provided by the information modeling system, and deriving and verifying relations between concepts according to the rules and various reasoning mechanisms. The operations support some mechanisms for maintaining, interpreting, and updating knowledge.

There are implicit links between information modeling, cognitive modeling and knowledge modeling. Constructivism argues that humans generate knowledge and meaning from some interactions between experiences and knowledge [94,139]. Learning with some styles is one type of such interactions [91].

The unconventional mapping is open as the information modeling system can also receive new information and models, the cognitive modeling system can get new definition of concepts, and rules from the external system, and the knowledge space modeling system can receive concepts, rules and structures from the external systems including other computing systems, humans, and society.

Human knowledge development may experience several stages according to developmental psychologists [94]: (1) *Sensorimotor stage* (from birth to age 2), when humans experience movement and their five senses. (2) *Preoperational stage* (from age 2 to 7), when humans learn to speak. (3) *Concrete operational stage* (from ages 7 to 11), when children can conserve and think logically but are limited to what they can physically manipulate. (4) *Formal operational stage* (from age 11 to 16 and onwards), when humans develop abstract reasoning, think abstractly, and use metacognition.

Simulating human knowledge development, the unconventional mapping can run with different stages: from one model to many models, from few rules to many rules, from few mechanisms to many mechanisms, and from one area to multiple areas.

16.5   Human-machine-nature symbiosis

Humans have worldviews, commonsense, motivation, knowledge (knowledge of representation and knowledge to be represented as discussed before), abstraction ability, analogical ability, experience and emotion, and can be inspired from reading representations like scientific papers in order to make creative summarizations. Moreover, the human mind works with a conscious system and a cooperative subconscious system to deal with various cases efficiently.

Machines do not have those abilities but they are good at searching necessary representations such as web pages and tweets, finding frequent patterns in big volumes of representations, carrying out simulation, and providing interactive interfaces.

One way to make a creative summarizer is to simulate cognitive infrastructure including the fundamental mechanism needed for creative summarization. Some prior knowledge and the ability to acquire knowledge can help automatic summarization system obtain certain creativity. This is involved in simulating cognitive

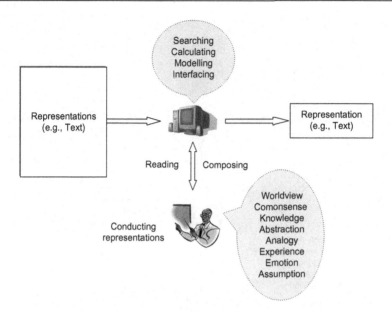

Figure 16.7 Human-machine symbiotic summarization.

infrastructure [107,122]. A complex space consisting of a multi-dimensional categorization space and a semantic link network was suggested as the fundamental structure for managing knowledge [139−141].

Another way is to establish a human-machine symbiotic summarization system
that can make use of both human intelligence and machine ability as depicted in
Figure 16.7. The key is to find the appropriate partners and the way to coordinate
them in real time. Personality is one measure of selection and can help determine
the way to coordinate men and machines. Machines will provide a draft summary
and natural interaction interface through searching, calculating and modeling, while
humans are responsible for final selection and revision according to worldview,
commonsense, knowledge, abstraction and analogy. Further, machines can learn
from interactions with humans and then do more works.

Different from machines, humans have social characteristics or behaviors including emotion, motivation, value, etc. The person who is willing to make summarizations is motivated within some communities in social networks, as shown in
Figure 16.8. When making summarizations, people can share knowledge, resolve
conflicts (in worldviews, understandings, interests, etc.), inspire each other, make
new friends, work in cooperation, and adjust summary according to justification on
knowledge and comments. Summarization is made through the execution of a symbiotic network of machines (Turing machines or new machines) and humans (with
individual and social intelligence).

A creative summarization system will show creativeness if it incorporates biological intelligence, machine intelligence, and social intelligence.

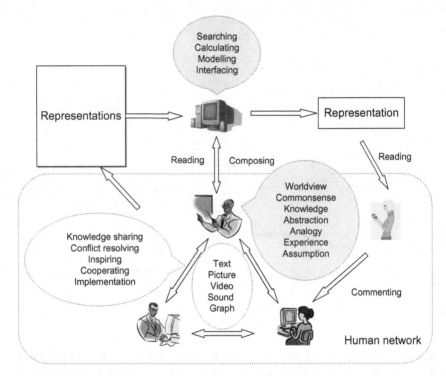

Figure 16.8 Human-machine symbiotic summarization in society.

16.6 Extend to brain

The human brain is the result of the long-term evolution of the nature. More advanced scientific equipments are able to capture more detailed data of brain. Brain data indicate human motivation and behaviors to a certain extent. Many countries and regions have invested in brain research. The USA's BRAIN initiative announced in 2013 aims at supporting the development and application of innovative technologies that can create a dynamic understanding of brain function. More and more brain data will be available in the future with the progress of exploring brain.

The brain evolves while reflecting the real world and instructing human behaviors including the operations of cyberspace. How to structure the cyberspace to optimize the interaction between human and cyberspace is important for developing cyberspace. Figure 16.9 depicts the relations among brain data space, knowledge space and cyberspace. The change of one space influences another space directly or indirectly. The change of cyberspace influences human operation behavior and knowledge space, and influences brain data. The change of brain data indicates the change of operation behaviors, which will influence cyberspace. The change of knowledge space influences the operation and the content of cyberspace.

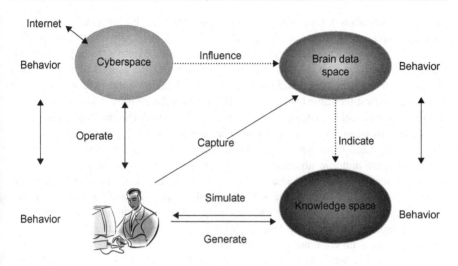

Figure 16.9 Symbiosis of cyberspace, brain data space, and knowledge space.

The following are three roles through which brain data is incorporated into the system.

(1) Estimate the motivation of operating cyberspace, such as searching and browsing.
(2) Identify the scope of interest and knowledge.
(3) Structure cyberspace suitable for human to operate.

The complex system consisting of cyberspace and social space will be efficient if cyberspace can be organized into a kind of external mind of human, which works harmoniously with the brain.

Summarization is a kind of high-level intelligence. It is interesting to build a summarization system that can make summarization while observing the characteristics of brain data space.

16.7   Incorporating learning theories and techniques

Summarization is a process of learning and using language. Generating dimensions from observation accompanies an understanding process, which is a process of mapping a representation at a certain level (e.g., natural language) into the multi-dimensional space in mind. As individuals have diversity in developing mental dimensions due to the difference of experience, different individuals may generate different dimensions on representing the same object [142].

The multi-dimensional categorization space assumption [134] is in line with learning studies. The Felder and Silverman model suggests that students learn along different dimensions: hearing and seeing, reflecting and acting, reasoning logically or intuitively, memorizing and visualizing, and drawing analogies [35]. Therefore teaching styles should vary with educators' preferences. This provides evidence of summarizing learning materials along multiple dimensions to help understanding. The variation theory of learning [70] suggests that teachers identify the aspects of the learning content and then use the patterns of variation in these aspects to help students to discern differences. The basic conjecture is that learning happens with discerning difference against the same background. The variation theory provides an evidence for designing significant dimensions that enable users to better know the original text.

In the computing area, a deep learning approach develops rapidly with the availability of big data. It allows computational models of multiple layers to learn representations with multiple abstraction levels. Deep learning approaches have shown some abilities in discovering some structures in large data sets with a back propagation algorithm to indicate how a machine should change its internal parameters for computing the representation of each layer from the representation of the lower layer. It is a natural idea to use deep learning approaches to understand texts. Major progress may come with combining representation learning with complex reasoning [60]. Deep learning is a useful tool for providing predictive solutions for big data analytics.

Deep learning has made great progress in processing images, videos, speeches, and audios. It is a natural idea to map text, image, speech, and audio into the same space through deep learning to realize a general summarization. An interesting issue is to learn the dimensions with abstraction hierarchy on big data while carrying out deep learning. However, deep learning is still empirical and lacks theory. It can be a model for processing big data but it is limited in its ability to represent knowledge and perform diverse reasoning required by intelligent systems. It is an incremental improvement of existing computing method rather than a revolutionary computing model.

16.8   The emotion dimension

Emotion is one dimension of summarizing texts, reflecting the state of feeling that influences behaviors. Emotion can also be regarded as a space with multiple dimensions, for example: *behavior* (*activation*, *deactivation*) and *feeling* (*pleasant*, *unpleasant*). Figure 16.10 depicts a scenario of summarization through a space with the emotion dimension. The emotional distance between different representations can be measured at the emotion dimension. Therefore, a summarization can be carried out while considering the emotion of the writer and the requirement of the reader. The emotion dimension is useful in summarizing works of literature and recommendations.

Vincent van Gogh (1853−1890) used a combination of poppies and other flowers he liked to symbolize his complex passion in the painting "Vase with Daisies and Poppies." He painted it in France in the year of his death. Fifteen years after, John McCrae (1872−1918) used poppies to represent memorial for the dead soldiers during the World War I in his memorial poem "In Flanders Fields" in 1915. Now, using poppies to commemorate sacrifice has become a part of culture in western countries. Putting artifacts into a space as shown in Figure 16.11 helps identify the emotion flow through times, which constructs the understanding basis. For example, the conception of the page illustrated by Ernest Clegg is similar to that of van Gogh's painting "Field of Poppies." There is no double that Ernest Clegg read

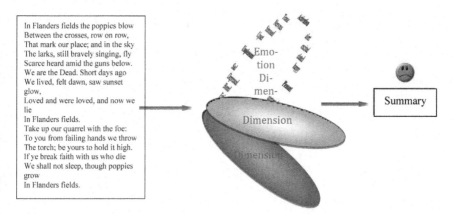

Figure 16.10 Summarization through mapping representations into the space with emotion dimension.

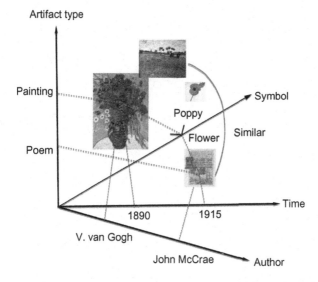

Figure 16.11 A multi-dimensional artifact space. "Vase with Daisies and Poppies," 1890 by Vincent van Gogh. "Field of Poppies," 1890 by Vincent van Gog. "In Flanders Fields," 1915, John McCrae.

the poem. Was he inspired from van Gogh? John McCrae and Ernest Clegg had a chance to see van Gogh's "Field of Poppies" in terms of time and geographical location (France and UK are close). If they were inspired by Vincent van Gogh's painting, we can see the emotion flow from van Gogh to John McCrae, to Ernest Clegg, and to the people who commemorate the sacrifice from generation to generation, and the evolution of the flow. If John McCrae did not see van Gogh's painting, they are likely to have the similar emotions inspired by the similar physical scene: the field of poppies.

Conclusion

The symbol space has been accompanying and reflecting the evolution of human society since the invention of languages. It is necessary to explore automatic summarization of various representations expanding rapidly in cyberspace, which will significantly transform the traditional symbol space. Summarizing the existing methods is the basis for understanding and creating methods. The existing methods are empirical, mainly relying on statistical, structural, and linguistic analysis while neglecting the nature of representation and understanding. It is important to explore the fundamental theory and method for summarization from multiple dimensions.

This research is carried out via the following basic viewpoints: the structure of a representation emerges with operations on it, a complex structure is near decomposable, and summarization with various interactions involved in human, machines, and various representations including texts, pictures, and videos. Writers and readers represent things as semantic images in mind and understand things mainly through explicit or implicit citations. A general summarization is a process of forming explicit and implicit citations. Investigating a general citation and the summarization of texts, pictures, videos, and graphs though the general citation provides instances for studying a general summarization method.

Generally, summarization is an open representation of representation, in diverse forms, from multiple dimensions, and through various interactions in multiple spaces. The basic interactions include selecting, understanding, citing and organizing representations according to requirement and motivation.

It is difficult for automatic summarization systems to realize human-level summarization, as it concerns the essential natural and social differences between humans and computing systems. A strategy is to make use of human summaries, which exist within the extensions of the thing to be summarised. Creating a human-level, cyber-concept mechanism is the basis for machine understanding. Realizing the unconventional mapping from data into knowledge is the foundation of realizing a creative summarization, which is based on knowledge of language use and knowledge to be represented.

The traditional paradigm of text processing is mainly application led, that is: Application with requirement (e.g., summarization with the scale requirement of summary) $\Rightarrow$ Method (find a method) $\Rightarrow$ Evaluation (with data). This book is an effort to transforming the traditional paradigm into a new paradigm of summarization, which is data led:

Data (e.g., text) $\Rightarrow$ Representation (e.g., reading, writing, and citing) $\Rightarrow$ Information Modeling—Cognitive Modeling—Knowledge Modeling $\Rightarrow$ Apply knowledge to applications (to meet requirements).

The foundation is the multi-dimensional think lens that can observe various representations (data, information, cognitive process and knowledge), make

Multi-Dimensional Summarization in Cyber-Physical Society. DOI: http://dx.doi.org/10.1016/B978-0-12-803455-2.00017-2

appropriate transformations between different representations through information modelling, cognitive modelling and knowledge modelling, and interpret based on reasoning. Multi-dimensional methodology supports research and development of summarization with insight. Developing summarization in the human-machine-nature symbiotic environment is another way to make a breakthrough. The Appendix A will introduce the basic concepts on human-machine-nature symbiosis. A significant progress of summarization research relies on an innovative summarization of philosophy, psychology, linguistics, cognitive science, physics, cyber-infrastructure, and artificial intelligence from multiple dimensions.

Studying the transformation of the research paradigm in the summarization area with cross-disciplinary inspiration provides a case study for exploring the methodology of data science and cyber-physical society [142].

Appendix A: Human—machine—nature symbiosis

A.1 Symbiosis

Symbiosis refers to a mutual benefit or dependence relationship established through long-term interactions between two or more biological species. A symbiosis mechanism refers to the living pattern of an organism in a natural ecosystem, which is the result of long-term evolution. It can improve the efficiency of using resources and reduce waste for natural ecosystems.

In nature, a symbiotic relationship can be either strong or weak. A strong symbiotic relation concerns the survival of species such as bees and flowers. Flowers seed because of bees, and bees generate honey because of flowers. Weak symbiosis exists widely in nature, for example, between crocodiles and plover birds, which benefit each other but do not heavily rely on each other.

Nature provides the material basis for the generation and development of living beings. Interactions between various individuals in natural physical spaces have generated and evolved many spaces. Human society is an example of such a space. In this case it refers to the physical space where humans live, work, and evolve. At the same time, artificial spaces of various forms are also created.

Thousands of years of social development has generated versatile social units such as communities and roles: one links to the other. Some links enable social units to benefit each other in the same manner as symbiosis in nature. For example, students and teachers constitute a symbiotic relation. Banks and customers constitute a symbiotic relation. Some customers save money in the bank and get interest while some borrow money from the bank and pay interest to the bank. The bank earns the difference on the interest. Customers can be involved in other symbiotic relations to form a symbiotic network. Suppliers, manufacturers, and consumers constitute a symbiotic relation. Deploying factories at appropriate locations so that some factories input the waste of the other factories constitutes industry symbiosis within the same region. Different from symbiosis in nature, symbiosis in society is artificial so it may not be as effective as natural symbiotic relations that have evolved for millions of years, and it forms a more complex symbiotic social network. For example, the industrial symbiotic network consists of information flow, material flow, energy flow, and money flow [1,2].

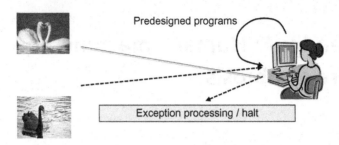

Figure A.1 Turing computing paradigm.

A.2 Turing computing paradigm

General-purpose computers are designed for solving problems or processing data according to procedures that are predetermined by humans. Almost all computers nowadays are essentially Turing machines [3]. One characteristic of a Turing machine is that all alternatives must be foreseen in advance.

Figure A.1 depicts the Turing computing paradigm, which manipulates symbols according to the rules given by humans. However, some problems can be difficult to think through in advance. For example, it is difficult for programmers who only have knowledge of white swans to imagine black swans.

A.3 Man–computer symbiosis

Licklider proposed man–computer symbiosis to enable computers to facilitate formulative thinking, and to enable men and computers to cooperate in making decisions and controlling complex situations without relying on predetermined programs. For man–computer symbiosis, men set goals, propose hypotheses, determine criteria, and carry out evaluations while computers perform the routine work that is necessary to prepare the way for insights and decisions in technical and scientific thinking. This symbiosis was expected to perform intellectual operations much more effectively than man alone can perform.[4] Although many pre-request techniques for realizing man–machine symbiosis have been realized, computers are still unable to participate in human real-time thinking, which involve such behaviors as searching, calculating, plotting, transforming, determining solutions, preparing for decisions, and considering feasibility.

Some techniques for bringing computing machines effectively into the formulative parts of problems still remain unsolved. Licklider's idea is still valuable today for developing advanced computing systems [5–7].

It's a great challenge to bring computing machines effectively into the processes of thinking. One difficulty is the detection of human thinking in real-time.

Human behaviors (e.g., conversation) reflect thinking to a certain extent, and most human behaviors are predictable. So a way to detect human thinking is to collect data about behaviors and predict thinking according to the relations between behaviors and thinking. The development of the Internet of Things provides techniques for collecting data about behaviors.

A.4   Human—Machine—Nature Symbiosis

The progress of human society has created an artifact space. Artifacts include tools, houses, roads, bridges, and various machines, which are objects in physical space and have functions and roles in social space. In 1969, Simon first proposed the idea of bridging physical domains and virtual domains [8], but it was ignored by the mainstream of computing research until the emergence of the Cyber-Physical Systems and the Internet of Things. However, there are some big gaps between cyberspace, physical space, and social space.

With the generation and development of information technology, cyberspace has been created to hold digital objects. The development of various sensors, mobile devices, and communication networks enables cyberspace to connect the physical space and social space to form a complex space. Interactions and behaviors in one space can influence the other spaces through various relations. Symbiosis is a basic relation of the complex space.

Figure A.2 depicts a scenario of Human—Machine—Nature Symbiosis [9]. Material flows, information flows, and control flows in space and between spaces form closed loops in the environment. Material flows include the flows of various materials required by the social space, irrigation, or fertilization.

The following are some characteristics of this environment:

(1) *Cyberspace can reflect more of the physical space and social space by using advanced sensors, actuators, interactive interfaces, and link situations in different spaces to provide cyber—physical—socio services.* For example, the scale of farming can link to the requirements of society.

(2) *Multi-dimensional real-time status about individuals and communities in the physical space and the social space can be captured.* For example, the status of crops concerns nutrient dimensions, health dimensions, function dimensions, economic dimensions, and time dimensions.

(3) *The cyber—physical—social effects of various behaviors are available so that appropriate decisions can be made to ensure harmonious development of various spaces.* For example, climate change in the physical space may influence agriculture, which may influence society.

(4) *The mental space will develop new functions as it will emerge and evolve new semantic images when reflecting multiple spaces simultaneously.* For example, people can view complex link networks in the social space and relevant real-time events in the physical space while reading or writing in the cyberspace. While drinking tea, people can know the characteristics of the tea and its production process from touch tablets or mobile devices, enjoy the tea-cultural performance in the physical space, verify the quality of the tea through the equipment linked to the tablet or mobile device, access the soil status of the tea trees in the physical space, and finally make a summarization about the tea.

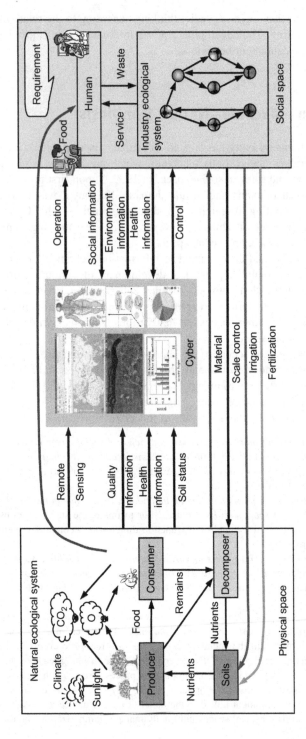

Figure A.2 The closed loops of links between cyberspace, physical space and social space.

(5) *Linking different spaces enables one space to make use of material, energy, and information in the other space.* For example, linking the agricultural ecological system to the industrial ecological system enables some waste of industry to be used as the fertilizer of crops, and enables the agricultural products to be the raw materials of some industries.

Influence through spaces can also form closed loops. Changes in physical space such as the increase of roads and buildings could influence cyberspace and the social space. Changes in the social space, such as a population increase, could influence the physical space and cyberspace. Changes in the social space and cyberspace could influence the interactions between humans, which influence the mental space. The change of mental space could change semantic images, which could influence behaviors in cyberspace, physical space, and the social space.

Human—machine—nature symbiosis is a study of various interactions among species (communities or certain classifications) in cyberspace, physical space, and social space, the impacts of interactions and changes, and the design and analysis of various symbiotic networks.

Human beings will live and harmoniously develop with various human—machine—nature symbiotic relations in the cyber—physical—social space. Understanding the fundamental structure of the complex space can inspire the creation of new computing paradigms. On the other hand, new challenges, such as security issues, emerge with the establishment of human—machine—nature symbiosis, as threats will be extended from cyberspace, the physical space, and social space through various links.

A.5   Summary

With the development of Cyber—Physical Society (Zhuge, 2012; [10]), computing will carry on in the complex space where various individuals in different spaces interact with each other through human—machine—nature symbiosis [9,11], which is the extension of the man—computer symbiosis proposed by Licklider. The idea of Human—Machine—Nature Symbiosis is valuable for developing computing systems and inspiring new computing paradigms. The Internet of Things provides the techniques for connecting cyberspace to the physical space and collecting data about various behaviors. Big data provide a chance for computing systems to predict the problems and discover knowledge to solve problems before programming [12].

Hai Zhuge
School of Engineering and Applied Science,
Aston University, Birmingham, UK

References

[1] M.R. Chertow, Industrial symbiosis: literature and taxonomy, Annu. Rev. Energy Environ. 25 (2000) 313—337.

[2] T.E. Graedel, B.R. Allenby, Industrial Ecology and Sustainable Engineering, Prentice Hall, Upper Saddle River, NJ, 2010.

[3] A. Turing, Computing machinery and intelligence, Mind 59 (236) (1950) 433–460.

[4] J.C.R. Licklider, Man-Computer Symbiosis, IRE Trans. Hum Factors Electron. HFE-1 (March 1960) 4–11.

[5] I. Foster, Human-Machine Symbiosis, 50 Years On, <arxiv.org/abs/0712.2255>.

[6] H. Zhuge, The Knowledge Grid: Toward the Cyber-Physical Society, first ed., World Scientific, Hackensack, NJ, 2004, 2012 (second ed.).

[7] H. Zhuge, The future interconnection environment, IEEE Computer 38 (4) (2005) 27–33.

[8] H.A. Simon, The Science of the Artificial, third ed., MIT Press, 1969, 1996.

[9] H. Zhuge, Semantic linking through spaces for Cyber-Physical-Socio intelligence: a methodology, Artif. Intell. 175 (2011) 988–1019.

[10] H. Zhuge, Multi-Dimensional Summarization in Cyber-Physical Society, Morgan Kaufmann, USA, 2016.

[11] H. Zhuge, Interactive semantics, Artif. Intell. 174 (2010) 190–204.

[12] H. Zhuge, Mapping big data into knowledge space with cognitive cyber-infrastructure. <arXiv:1507.06500>, 24 July 2015.

[13] H. Zhuge, X. Shi, Toward the eco-grid: a harmoniously evolved interconnection environment, Commun. ACM 47 (9) (2004) 78–83.

References

[1] S. Afantenos, V. Karkaletsis, P. Stamatopoulos, Summarization from medical documents: a survey, Artif. Intell. Med. 33 (2) (2005) 157–177.

[2] R. Agrawal, S. Gollapudi, A. Kannan, K. Kenthapadi, Enriching textbooks with images, in: Proceedings of the 20th ACM International Conference on Information and Knowledge Management, UK, 2011, pp. 1847–1856.

[3] N. Agarwal, K. Gvr, R.S. Reddy, C.P. Rosé, SciSumm: a multi-document summarization system for scientific articles, in: Proceedings of the ACL-HLT 2011 System Demonstrations, USA, 2011, 115–120.

[4] A. Abu-Jbara, D. Radev, Coherent citation-based summarization of scientific papers, in: HLT '11 Proceedings of the 49th Annual Meeting of the Association for Computational Linguistics: Human Language Technologies – Volume 1, USA, 2011, 500–509.

[5] M. Ashburner, et al., Gene ontology: tool for the unification of biology, Nat. Genet. 25 (2000) 25–29.

[6] J.R. Anderson, Cognitive Psychology and Its Implications, Seventh ed., Worth Publishers, New York, 2010.

[7] R. Barzilay, M. Elhadad, Using lexical chains for text summarization, in: Proceedings of ISTS'97, Japan, 1997.

[8] R. Barzilay, K.R. McKeown, M. Elhadad, Information fusion in the context of multi-document summarization, in: Proceedings of ACL'99, USA, 1999.

[9] R. Barzilay, K. McKeown, Sentence fusion for multidocument news summarization, Comput. Linguist. 31 (3) (2005) 297–328.

[10] R. Barzilay, M. Lapata, Modeling local coherence: an entity-based approach, Comput. Linguist. 1 (34) (2008) 1–34.

[11] P. Baxendale, Machine-made index for technical literature – an experiment, IBM J. Res. Dev. 2 (4) (1958) 354–361.

[12] E. Bates, F. Dick, Language, gesture, and the developing brain, Dev. Psychobiol. 40 (2002) 293–310.

[13] R. Brandow, K. Mitze, L.F. Rau, Automatic consideration of electronic publications by sentence selection, Inf. Process. Manage. 5 (31) (1995) 675–685.

[14] B.K. Britton, A.C. Graesser (Eds.), Models of understanding text, Psychology Press, Taylor & Francis Group, New York and London, 1996.

[15] J. Carbonell, J. Goldstein, The use of MMR, diversity-based reranking for reordering documents and producing summaries, in: Proceedings of ACM SIGIR'98, Australia, 1998, pp. 335–336.

[16] S. Ceccato, Linguistic Analysis and Programming for Mechanical Translation, Gordon and Breach, New York, 1961.

[17] B.-W. Chen, J.-C. Wang, J.-F. Wang, A novel video summarization based on mining the story-structure and semantic relations among concept entities, IEEE Trans. Multimedia 11 (2) (2009) 295–312.

[18] J. Chen, H. Zhuge, Summarization of scientific documents by detecting common facts in citations, Future Gener. Computer Syst. 32 (2014) 246–252.

[19] C.L.A. Clarke, et al., Novelty and diversity in information retrieval evaluation, in: Proceedings of ACM SIGIR'08, Singapore, 2008, pp. 659–666.

[20] N. Chomsky, Language and Mind, third ed., Cambridge University Press, Cambridge, 2006.

[21] N. Chomsky, Knowledge of Language: Its Nature, Origin, and Use, Praeger Publisher, New York, 1986.

[22] A.M. Collins, E.F. Loftus, A spreading-activation theory of semantic processing, Psychol. Rev. 82 (6) (1975) 407–428.

[23] J.M. Conroy, D.P. O'leary, Text summarization via hidden markov models, in: Proceedings of SIGIR, USA, 2001, 406-407.

[24] G. Cormode, S. Muthukrishnan, An improved data stream summary: the count-min sketch and its applications, J. Algorithms 55 (1) (2005) 58–75.

[25] H. Daumé III, D. Marcu, A tree-position kernel for document compression, in: Proceedings of DUC2004, USA, 2004.

[26] H. Daumé III, D. Marcu, Bayesian query-focused summarization, in: Proceedings of ACL-2006, France, 2006, 305–312.

[27] R. Davis, B. Buchanan, E. Shortliffe, Production rules as a representation for a knowledge-based consultation program, Artif.l intell. 8 (1) (1977) 15–45.

[28] D. DeMenthon, V. Kobla, D. Doermann, Video summarization by curve simplification, in: Proceedings of the 6th ACM International Conference on Multimedia, UK, 1998, pp. 211–218.

[29] H.P. Edmundson, New methods in automatic extracting, J. ACM 16 (1969) 23–42.

[30] A. Elkiss, et al., Blind men and elephants: what do citation summaries tell us about a research article? J. Am. Soc. Infor. Sci. Technol. Arch. 59 (1) (2008) 51–62.

[31] A. Elkiss, S. Shen, A. Fader, Lexrank: graphbased lexical centrality as salience in text summarization, J. Artif. Intell. Res. 22 (2004) 457–479.

[32] A. Ekin, A.M. Tekalp, R. Mehrotra, Automatic soccer video analysis and summarization, IEEE Trans. Image Process. 12 (7) (2003) 796–807.

[33] K.A. Ericsson, W. Kintsch, Long-term working memory, Psychol. Rev. 102 (2) (1995) 211–245.

[33a] G. Erkan, D.R. Radev, LexRank: graph-based lexical centrality as salience in text summarization, J. Artif. Intell. Res. 22 (2004) 457–479.

[34] M.A. Fattah, A hybrid machine learning model for multi-document summarization, Appl. Intell. 40 (4) (2014) 592–600.

[35] R.M. Felder, L.K. Silverman, Learning and teaching styles in engineering education, Eng. Educ. 78 (7) (1988) 674–681.

[36] C.R. Fletcher, C.P. Bloom, Causal reasoning in the comprehension of simple narrative texts, J. Mem. lang. 26 (1988) 69–83.

[37] A.D. Friederici, M. Meyer, D.Y.V. Cramon, Auditory language comprehension: an event-related fmri study on the processing of syntactic and lexical information, Brain and Lang. 74 (2) (2000) 289–300.

[38] M. Friedman, A.Y. Levy, T.D. Millstein, Navigational plans for data integration, in: Proceedings of AAAI, USA, pp. 67–73, 1999.

[39] Jerry A. Fodor, , The Modularity of Mind: An Essay on Faculty Psychology, MIT Press, Cambridge, MA, 1983.

[40] M. Foucault, The Order of Things, Gallimard, Paris, 1966.

[41] M. Foucault, First published by Editions The Archaeology of Knowledge, Gallimard, Paris, 1969.

[42] E. Gibson, Linguistic complexity: locality of syntactic dependencies, Cognition 68 (1) (1998) 1−76.

[43] Y. Gong, X. Liu, Generic text summarization using relevance measure and latent semantic analysis, in: ACM SIGIR, USA, 2001, 19−25.

[44] L.A. Gottschalk, G.C. Gleser, The Measurement of Psychological States Through the Content Analysis of Verbal Behavior, University of California Press, Berkeley, CA, 1969.

[45] A.C. Graesser, M. Singer, T. Trabasso, Constructing inferences during narrative text comprehension, Psychol. Rev. 101 (1994) 371−395.

[46] A.C. Graesser, K. Millis, R.A. Zwaan, Discourse comprehension, Annu. Rev. Psychol. 48 (1997) 163−189.

[47] O. Gross, A. Doucet, H. Toivonen, Document summarization based on word association, in: Proceedings of ACM SIGIR, Australia, 2014.

[48] V.N. Gudivada, V.V. Raghavan, Content based image retrieval systems, Computer 9 (28) (1995) 18−22.

[49] J. Gray, What next?: a dozen information-technology research goals, J. ACM 50 (1) (2003) 41−57.

[50] T.R. Gruber, A translation approach to portable ontology specifications, Knowl. Acquis. 5 (2)) (1993) 199−220.

[51] U. Hahn, The challenges of automatic summarization, Computer 33 (11) (2000) 29−36.

[52] H. Hardy, N. Shimizu, T. Strzalkowski, L. Ting, X. Zhang, G.B. Wise, Cross-document summarization by concept classification, in: ACM SIGIR, Finland, 2002, 121−128.

[53] A. Halevy, A. Rajaraman, J. Ordille, Data integration: the teenage years, Proceedings of the 32nd International Conference on Very Large Data Bases (VLDB), Korea, 2006, pp. 9−16.

[54] J. Hornak, E.T. Rolls, D. Wade, Face and voice expression identification in patients with emotional and behavioural changes following ventral frontal lobe damage, Neuropsychologia 34 (4) (1996) 247−261.

[55] M. Hu, B. Liu, Mining and summarizing customer reviews, in: Proceedings of ACM KDD, USA, 2004, 168−177.

[56] W. Kintsch, T.A.V. Dijk, Toward a model of text comprehension and production, Psychol. Rev. 85 (5) (1978) 363−394.

[57] K. Knight, D. Marcu, Summarization beyond sentence extraction: a probabilistic approach to sentence compression, Artif. Intell. 139 (1) (2002) 91−107.

[58] J. Kupiec, J. Pedersen, F. Chen, A trainable document summarizer. in: Proceedings SIGIR'95, New York, 1995, pp. 68−73.

[59] D. LaBerge, S.J. Samuels, Toward a theory of automatic information processing in reading, Cognitive Psychol. 6 (1974) 293−323.

[60] Y. LeCun, Y. Bengio, G. Hinton, Deep learning, Nature 521 (2015) 436−444.

[61] D.B. Lenat, E.A. Feigenbaum, On the thresholds of knowledge, Artif. intell. 47 (1−3) (1991) 185−250.

[62] J.C.R. Licklider, Man-computer symbiosis, IRE Trans. Hum. Factors Electron. HFE-1 (1960) 4−11.

[63] C.-Y. Lin, Rouge: a package for automatic evaluation of summaries, in text summarization branches out. in: Proceedings of the ACL-04 Workshop, Spain, 2004.

[64] C.-Y. Lin, E. Hovy, Automatic evaluation of summaries using n-gram co-occurrence statistics, in: Proceedings of the 2003 Conference of the North American Chapter of the Association for Computational Linguistics on Human Language Technology, Volume 1, USA, 2003, pp. 71−78.

[65] S. Liu, M.X. Zhou, S. Pan, Y. Song, W. Qian, W. Cai, et al., TIARA: interactive, topic-based visual text summarization and analysis, ACM Trans. Intell. Syst. Technol. 3 (2) (2012), article no. 25.

[66] G.R. Loftus, N.H. Mackworth, Cognitive determinants of fixation location during picture viewing, J. Exp. Psychol.: Hum. Percept. Perform. 4 (4) (1978) 565−572.

[67] A. Louis, A Bayesian method to incorporate background knowledge during automatic text summarization, in: Proceedings of ACL, USA, 2014.

[68] M. Lenzerini, Data integration: a theoretical perspective, in: Proceedings of the 21st ACM SIGMOD-SIGACT-SIGART Symposium on Principles of Database Systems (PDOS), USA, 2002, pp. 233−246.

[69] H.P. Luhn, The automatic creation of literature abstracts, IBM J. Res. Dev. 2 (1958) 159−165.

[70] F. Marton, et al., Classroom Discourse and the Space of Learning, Routledge, Taylor & Francis Group, New York, NY 10017, 2004.

[71] A.H. Maslow, A theory of human motivation, Psychol. Rev. 50 (4) (1943) 370−396.

[72] J. McCarthy, From here to human-level AI, Artif. Intell. 171 (18) (2007) 1174−1182.

[73] J. McCarthy, The well-designed child, Artif. Intell. 172 (18) (2008) 2003−2014.

[74] I. Mani, M.T. Maybury, Advances in Automatic Text Summarization, MIT Press, Cambridge, MA, 1999.

[75] I. Mani, Automatic Summarization, John Benjamins B.V., Amsterdam, The Netherlands, 2001.

[76] W.C. Mann, S.A. Thompson, Rhetorical structure theory: toward a functional theory of text organization, Interdiscip. J. Study Discourse 8 (3) (1988) 243−281.

[77] K.R. McKeown, D.R. Radev, Generating summaries of multiple news articles, in: Proceedings of ACM SIGIR'95, 1995, USA, pp. 74−82.

[78] K.R. McKeown, et al., Towards multidocument summarization by reformulation: progress and prospects, in: Proceedings of AAAI-99, USA, 1999.

[79] R. Mihalcea, P. Tarau, TextRank: bringing order into texts, in: Proceedings of EMNLP 2004, Barcelona, Spain, 2004, pp. 404−411.

[80] R. Mihalcea, Language independent extractive summarization, in: Proceedings of AAAI, USA, 2005, 1688−1689.

[81] M. Minsky, A framework for representing knowledge, in: P. Winston (Ed.), The Psychology of Computer Vision, McGraw-Hill, New York, 1975.

[82] M. Minsky, The Emotion Machine: Commonsense Thinking, Artificial Intelligence, and the Future of the Human Mind, *Simon & Schuster*, New York, 2006.

[83] G.L. Murphy, The Big Book of Concepts, MIT Press, Cambridge, MA, 2002.

[84] H. Nanba, M. Okumura, Towards multi-paper summarization using reference information, in: Proceedings of IJCAI, Sweden, 1999, 926−931.

[85] A. Nenkova, Automatic text summarization of newswire: Lessons learned from the document understanding conference, in: Proceedings of AAAI, 2005, Pttsburgh, PA.

[86] T. Nelson, L. Narens, Meta-memory: a theoretical treatment and new findings, in: G. Bower (Ed.), The Psychology of Learning and Motivation, vol. 26, Academic Press, New York, 1990.

[87] S. Navlakha, R. Rastoji, N. Shrivastava, Graph summarization with bounded error, in: Proceedings of ACM SIGMOD, Canada, 2008, 419−432.

[88] A. Newell, The knowledge level, Artif. Intell. 18 (1982) 87−127.

[89] M.E.J. Newman, Modularity and community structure in networks, Proc. Natl. Acad. Sci. USA 103 (23) (2006) 8577−8582.

[90] M.A. Nowak, K. Sigmund, Evolution of indirect reciprocity, Nature 427 (27) (2005) 1291–1298.

[91] H. Pashler, M. McDaniel, D. Rohrer, R. Bjork, Learning styles: concepts and evidence, Psychol. Sci. Public Interest 9 (3) (2009) 105–119.

[92] B. Pang, L. Lee, A sentimental education: sentiment analysis using subjectivity summarization based on minimum cuts, in: Proceedings of ACL, Spain, 2004, Article No. 271.

[93] S.V. Paunonen, M.C. Ashton, Big five factors and facets and the prediction of behavior, J. Pers. Soc. Psychol. 81 (3) (2001) 524–539.

[94] J. Piaget, The Origins of Intelligence in Children, Routledge and Kegan Paul, London, 1953.

[95] V. Qazvinian, D.R. Radev, Scientific paper summarization using citation summary networks, in: COLING '08 Proceedings of the 22nd International Conference on Computational Linguistics, vol. 1, UK, 2008, 689–696.

[96] V. Qazvinian, D.R. Radev. Identifying non-explicit citing sentences for citation-based summarization, in: Proceedings of ACL, Sweden, 2010, 555–564.

[97] M.R. Quillian, Semantic Memory, PhD dissertation, Carnegie Institute of Technology (now CMU), Pittsburgh, PA, 1966.

[98] D.R. Radev, K.R. Mckeown, Generating natural language summaries from multiple on-line sources, Comput. Linguist. 24 (3) (1998) 469–500.

[99] G. Raschia, N. Mouaddib, SAINTETIQ: a fuzzy set-based approach to database summarization, Fuzzy Sets and Syst. 129 (2) (2002) 137–162.

[100] L.F. Rau, P.S. Jacobs, U. Zernik, Information extraction and text summarization using linguistic knowledge acquisition, Inf. Process. Manage. 25 (4) (1989) 419–428.

[101] E.D. Reichle, A. Pollatsek, D.L. Fisher, K. Rayner, Toward a model of eye movement control in reading, Psychol. Rev. 105 (1) (1998) 125–157.

[102] K. Rayner, Eye movements in reading and information processing: 20 years of research, Psychol. Bull. 124 (3) (1998) 372–422.

[103] E. Rosch, C.B. Mervis, W.D. Gray, D.M. Johnson, P. Boyes-Braem, Basic objects in natural categories, Cognit. Psychol. 8 (3) (1976) 382–439.

[104] G. Salton, A. Wong, C.S. Yang, A vector space model for automatic indexing, Commun. ACM 18 (11) (1975) 613–620.

[105] G. Salton, A. Singhal, M. Mitra, C. Buckley, Automatic text structuring and summarization, Inf. Process. Manage. 33 (2) (1997) 193–207.

[106] R. Saint-Paul, G. Raschia, N. Mouaddib, General purpose database summarization, in: Proceedings of VLDB, Norway, 2005, 733–744.

[107] J.W. Schooler, S. Ohlsson, K. Brooks, Thoughts beyond words: when language overshadows insights, J. Exp. Psychol. Gen. 122 (2) (1993) 166–183.

[108] D. Shen, J.-T. Sun, H. Li, Q. Yang, Z. Chen, Document summarization using conditional random fields, in: Proceedings of IJCAI, 2007, 2862–2867.

[109] H.G. Silber, K.F. McCoy, Efficiently computed lexical chains as an intermediate representation for automatic text summarization, Comput. Linguist. 28 (4) (2002) 487–496.

[110] H.A. Simon, The Science of the Artificial, first ed., MIT Press, Cambridge, MA, 1969, 1977 (second ed.), 1996 (third ed.).

[111] N. Shroff, P. Turaga, R. Chellappa, Video précis: highlighting diverse aspects of videos, IEEE Trans. Multimedia 12 (8) (2010) 853–868.

[112] R.F. Simmons, Synthetic language behavior, Data Process. Manage. 5 (12) (1963) 11–18.

[113] D.N. Stern, Interpersonal World of the Infant: A view from psychoanalysis and devel-
       opment psychology, Basic Books, New York, 1985.
[114] Y.R. Tausczik, J.W. Pennebaker, The psychological meaning of words: LIWC and
       computerized text analysis methods, J. Lang. Soc. Psychol. 29 (1) (2009) 24−54.
[115] S. Teufel, Summarizing scientific articles: experiments with relevance and rhetorical
       status, Comput. Linguist. 28 (4) (2002) 409−445.
[115a] T. Trabasso, P.V.D. Broek, Causal thinking and the representation of narrative events,
       J. Mem. Lang. 24 (5) (1985) 612−630.
[116] T. Trabasso, L.L. Sperry, Causal relatedness and importance of story events, J. Mem.
       Lang. 24 (1985) 595−611.
[117] J. Nam, A.H. Tewfik, Dynamic video summarization and visualization, in:
       Proceedings of ACM Multimedia, 1999, 53−56.
[118] J.B. Tenenbaum, C. Kemp, T.L. Griffiths, N.D. Goodman, How to grow a mind:
       statistics, structure, and abstraction, Science 331 (6022) (2011) 1279−1285.
[119] Y. Tian, R.A. Hankins, J.M. Patel, Efficient aggregation for graph summarization, in:
       Proceedings of ACM SIGMOD, Canada, 2008, 567−580.
[120] P.E. Turkeltaub, G.F. Eden, K.M. Jones, T.A. Zeffiro, Meta-analysis of the functional
       neuroanatomy of single-word reading: method and validation, NeuroImage 16 (3)
       (2002) 765−780, Part A.
[121] N. UzZaman, J.P. Bigham, J.F. Allen, Multimodal summarization of complex sen-
       tences. in: Proceedings of the 16th ACM International Conference on Intelligent User
       Interfaces, Cyprus, 2011, pp. 43−52.
[122] G. Wallas, The Art of Thought, New York, Harcourt, Brace and Company, 1926.
[123] D. Wang, S. Zhu, T. Li, Y. Gong, Comparative document summarization via discrimi-
       native sentence selection, ACM Trans. Knowl. Discov. Data 6 (3) (2012), article no. 12.
[124] Y. Wilks, Getting meaning into the machine, IEEE Intell. Syst. 21 (3) (2006) 70−71.
[125] Y. Wilks, D. Fass, The preference semantics family, Comput. Math. Appl. 23 (2−5)
       (1992) 205−221.
[126] Y. Wilks, What sort of taxonomy of causation do we need for language understand-
       ing? Cogniti. Sci. 1 (3) (1977) 235−264.
[127] Y. Wilks, A preferential, pattern-seeking, semantics for natural language inference,
       Artif. Intell. 6 (1) (1975) 53−74.
[128] B. Xu, H. Zhuge, Faceted navigation through keyword interaction, World Wide Web
       17 (4) (2014) 671−689.
[129] B. Xu, H. Zhuge, A text scanning mechanism simulating human reading process, in:
       Proceedings of IJCAI, Beijing, 2013.
[130] R.R. Yager, A. New, Approach to the summarization of data, Inf. Sci. 28 (1) (1982)
       69−86.
[131] N. Zhang, Y. Tian, J.M. Patel, Discovery-driven graph summarization, Proceedings of
       IEEE ICDE, USA, 2010, pp. 880−891.
[132] X. Zhu, A.B. Goldberg, M. Eldawy, C.R. Dyer, B.Strock, A text-to-picture synthesis system
       for augmenting communication, Proceedings of AAAI, vol. 7, USA, 2007, 1590−1595.
[133] H. Zhuge, Active e-document framework ADF: model and tool, Inf. Manage. 41 (1)
       (2003) 87−97.
[134] H. Zhuge, The Web Resource Space Model, Springer, Berlin, 2008.
[135] H. Zhuge, Discovery of knowledge flow in science, Commun. ACM 49 (5) (2006)
       101−107.
[136] H. Zhuge, Y. Xing, P. Shi, Resource space model, OWL and database: mapping and
       integration, ACM Trans. Internet Technol. 8/4 (2008).

[137] H. Zhuge, Y. Xing, Probabilistic resource space model for managing resources in Cyber-Physical Society, IEEE Trans. Serv. Comput. 5 (3) (2012) 404−421.

[138] H. Zhuge, Communities and emerging semantics in semantic link network: discovery and learning, IEEE Trans. Knowl. Data Eng. 21 (6) (2009) 785−799.

[139] H. Zhuge, Interactive semantics, Artif. Intell. 174 (2) (2010) 190−204.

[140] H. Zhuge, Semantic linking through spaces for cyber-physical-socio intelligence: a methodology, Artif. Intell. 175 (2011) 988−1019.

[141] H. Zhuge, The Knowledge Grid — Toward the Cyber-Physical Society, second ed., Springer, Berlin, 2012 (2004, first ed.).

[142] H. Zhuge, Dimensionality on summarization, arXiv:1507.00209 [cs.CL], 2 July 2015.

[143] H. Zhuge, Mapping big data into knowledge space with cognitive cyber-infrastructure, arXiv:1507.06500, 24 July 2015.

[144] A. Zubiaga, D. Spina, E. Amigo, J. Gonzalo, Towards real-time summarization of scheduled events from twitter streams, in: Proceedings of ACM HT2012, USA, 2012, pp. 319−320.

[145] G. Erkan, D.R. Radev, LexRank: Graph-based lexical centrality as salience in text summarisation, Journal of Artificial Intelligence Research, 22 (2004) 457−479.

Printed in the United States
By Bookmasters